# Youth's Passage Through School To Work

**COMPLIMENTARY COPY
NOT FOR RESALE**

*This book may be ordered from:*

**THOMPSON Educational Publishing, Inc.**

*Publishing for the Social Sciences and the Humanities*
11 Briarcroft Road, TORONTO, ONTARIO M6S 1H3
Telephone (416) 766-2763 / Fax: (416) 766-0398

A companion volume by Stewart Crysdale entitled *Families Under Stress* is available from the publisher. Both studies were conducted in the same area of downtown Toronto, Ontario

This book has been published with the help of a grant from the Social Science Federation of Canada, using funds provided by the Social Sciences and Humanities Research Council of Canada.

# Youth's Passage Through School To Work

## *A Comparative, Longitudinal Study of Eastside, Canada*

**Stewart Crysdale**
*York University*

**Harry MacKay**
*Consultant, Social Research, Ottawa*

**THOMPSON EDUCATIONAL PUBLISHING, INC.**
*Toronto*

Copyright © 1994 Stewart Crysdale and Harry MacKay

All rights reserved. No part of this publication may be reproduced or transmitted in any form or by any means, electronic or mechanical, including photocopy, recording, or any information storage and retrieval system, without permission in writing from the publisher.

Requests for permission to make copies of any part of the work should be directed to the publisher. Additional copies of this book may be obtained from the publisher.

| *Canada* | or | *United States* |
|---|---|---|
| 14 Ripley Avenue, Suite 105 | | 240 Portage Road |
| Toronto, Ontario | | Lewiston, New York |
| M6S 3N9 | | 14092 |

Please place your order by telephone or fax to:
Tel (416) 766–2763 / Fax (416) 766–0398


Canadian Cataloguing in Publication Data
Crysdale, Stewart.
   Youth's passage through school to work

Includes bibliographical references.
ISBN 1-55077-048-9

1. Youth - Employment - Ontario - Toronto Metropolitan Area - Longitudinal studies.
2. Youth - Education - Ontario - Toronto Metropolitan Area - Longitudinal Studies. I Title.

HD6276.C33T63  1994      305.23'5'09713541    C94-094699-5


Photographs by Marlo Fieldstone, John Dawson and Stewart Crysdale.


Printed in Canada.
1  2  3     95 94

# Contents

|  |  |
|---|---|
| *Tables and Figures* | vii |
| *Preface and Acknowledgments* | ix |
| *Map of Eastside* | xii |

**1. Youth's Status Passage** — 3
- Research Design and Samples — 5
- Reasons for Leaving or Staying — 10
- Relevant Studies: Impact on Public Policy — 12

**2. Experiences in Early and Mid-Adolescence** — 16
- Background — 17
- Early Socialization — 23

**3. Intermediate Outcomes** — 35
- Aspirations for Education and Occupation — 36
- Expectations: The Reality Gap — 38
- Psychometric Test Scores — 39
- Ethnicity and Intermediate Outcomes — 41

**4. Late Adolescence** — 45
- Educational Attainment — 45
  - (a) School Completion and Drop-out Rates — 45
  - (b) The Fallacy of Tracking — 48
- Occupational Entry — 49

**5. The Intervention Programs** — 57
- Development and Participation — 57
- Results in Mid-Adolescence — 60
- Results in Late Adolescence — 61
- Effects in Young Adulthood — 66

**6. Entry Job and Satisfaction** — 68
- Path Models of Attainment — 68
- Job Satisfaction — 72
- Implications for Theory and Policy — 73

| | | |
|---|---|---|
| 7. | **Values, Beliefs and Attainment** | **77** |
| | Normative Variables in Two Areas | 78 |
| | Types of Ideologues | 80 |
| | Orientations and Correlates: Eastside Sketches | 81 |
| | Summary: Values of Downtown Youth | 88 |
| | Orientations and Correlates: Northtown Sketches | 89 |
| | Summary: Values of Uptown Youth | 97 |
| | Mobility Outcomes, by Ideological Type | 98 |
| 8. | **Summary, Conclusions and Recommendations** | **103** |
| | Summary | 103 |
| | Conclusions and Recommendations | 109 |

**Appendices**

| | |
|---|---|
| A: Young Adult Sample, Background by Area | 116 |
| B: Downtown Young Adults, Zero-Order Correlations | 117 |
| C: Uptown Young Adults, Zero-Order Correlations | 118 |
| D: Acronyms for Appendices B and C | 119 |

**References**     **121**

# Tables and Figures

**Figure 1-1:** Stage Model of the Passage of Youth through School into Work     6

**Table 1-1:** Interviews by Subsample in Successive Surveys (Percentages of 1969 Numbers Downtown and 1972 Uptown)     8

**Table 2-1:** Family Income, by Downtown Experimental and Control, and Uptown Control Groups, in Mid-Adolescence     19

**Table 2-2:** Father's Ethnicity, for Three Youth Samples, Mid-Adolescence     22

**Table 2-3:** Perceived Positive Parental Influence, by Downtown Early and Mid-Adolescents     25

**Table 2-4:** Perceived Positive Influence of Teachers, by Downtown Early and Mid-Adolescents     27

**Table 2-5:** Changes in Perception of Others as Most Influential, by Downtown Early and Mid-Adolescents     28

**Table 3-1:** Educational Aspiration of Downtown and Uptown Youth Samples, by Age     37

**Table 3-2:** Gap between Educational Aspirations and Expectations for College or University Graduation, for Three Youth Samples     39

**Table 3-3:** High Psychometric Test Scores of Downtown and Uptown Mid-Adolescents (16 to 18 Years Old)     40

**Table 4-1:** Educational Attainment of Out-of-School, Late Adolescent Samples     46

**Table 4-2:** Reasons for Completing or Leaving School, by Downtown and Uptown Late Adolescents     47

| | | |
|---|---|---|
| **Table 4-3:** | Factor Matrix of School Variables for Downtown Mid-Adolescents | 48 |
| **Table 4-4:** | Differences in the Work Characteristics of 18- to 20-Year-Old Full-Time Workers, Downtown and Uptown | 50 |
| **Table 4-5:** | Self-Confidence at Two Stages of Adolescence, Downtown and Uptown Samples | 53 |
| **Table 5-1:** | Young Adults Taking Courses, by Three Subsamples and by Sex | 66 |
| **Table 6-1:** | Downtown Young Adults, Significant Variables Regressed on Educational Attainment | 69 |
| **Table 6-2:** | Downtown Young Adults, Significant Variables Regressed on Job Level | 70 |
| **Table 6-3:** | Uptown Young Adults, Significant Variables Regressed on Educational Level | 71 |
| **Table 6-4:** | Uptown Young Adults, Significant Variables Regressed on Job Level | 72 |
| **Table 7-1:** | Normative Orientations, Two Areas, Late Adolescents | 78 |
| **Table 7-2:** | Types of Ideology in Two Areas, Youth Aged 21-23 | 80 |
| **Table 7-3:** | Career/Lifestyle Outcomes by Ideological Type, Downtown and Uptown Young Adults, In-depth Interviews | 99 |

# Preface and Acknowledgments

The Eastside Youth Project, spanning seventeen years, is a pioneering investigation in Canada of the transition of youth into work. It combines longitudinal survey and ethnographic methods, revealing the feelings as well as experiences of youth growing up in a changing metropolis. It addresses a critical national issue: the preparation of a competent young labour force to help Canada cope in a fiercely competitive world market. Finally, it assesses the accomplishments and limitations of an innovative intervention to assist disprivileged young people at a critical stage in their development. The report concludes with recommendations for strengthening ties between family, school and workplace so as to improve the passage into a productive and satisfying adulthood.

The findings are more relevant now than when the project began twenty-five years ago, especially for educators, employers, parents, youth and policy makers. At that time it was widely believed that the transition into work could be left to individuals. Only recently have influential persons begun to recognize the intransigent structures that, for a large portion of the emerging work force, block the way toward job satisfaction and productivity.

Progress has been made in public awareness but only modest accommodations have occurred in bridging education and employment. A positive initiative is wider availability of cooperative education, mostly in high school. But the vast majority of students still have vague ideas about future careers and how to achieve them. Less than ten percent of students are in co-op education; the rest are left on their own to find the way. There is no evidence that the drop-out rate across Canada has fallen from about 30 percent for at least two decades or that it has abated from twice that level in low-income areas.

Publication of this report has been delayed largely by the absence of funding for longitudinal research. The authors have been absorbed in full time jobs while completing this and other research projects. Because of the cost and difficulties attending longitudinal research, there is a dearth of studies on the effectiveness and limitations of intervention to aid youth in transition and to renew a viable work force. This volume helps to fill that void.

We are grateful for the generosity of many participants, beginning with 467 youth, most of whom were interviewed repeatedly over twelve years beginning in elementary school. They were remarkably honest, sometimes humorous and at times resentful and angry. School personnel accepted us as well-meaning observers of their inner world. Parents and community leaders helped in many ways. Employers provided funds, part-time jobs, counselling and organizational know-how. Public and private agencies supported us as we struggled to stay alive from year to year. Academic colleagues tried to save us from gross folly.

Scores of Atkinson College students at York University earned credits and vast experience as they searched for fast-moving subjects and interviewed them in their homes. In early phases University of Toronto graduate students helped by tutoring high school students. York administered the budget, the Institute of Social Research provided research services, the Atkinson sociology department took on extra duties cheerfully, and Hazel O'Loughlin and Rita Marinucci prepared the manuscript for publication.

Among those who worked creatively in the field, we can mention only a few. Youth included John diSalle, Sally Eden, Heather Fearon, Laurie Fryer, Bud Hammond, Paul Hanczer, Angelo Iounidis, Donna LaBarge, Donna Overholt, Dan Owen, Catherine Parsons, David Ralph, Sirkka Roman, Don Salichuck, John Taylor and Jean Tom. Among the parents were Joan Crawley and Pat Riley. Employers who gave sustained support included Sid Fraser and John Lockwood of Lever, Cec Kellough of Colgate-Palmolive, and Ross MacKenzie of Consumers Gas. Among educators who consistently helped were Superintendent Bill Sweetman, Director Ron Jones, Principals Bill Buddenhagen and Aubrey Rhamey, and Counsellor Barbara Burns. Bill Sutton of the City Planning Board and John Kinley of the Ontario Department of Labour were indispensable on the Board, and Edna Chojnaska and Bev Gander from Canada Manpower were more than generous. Among community leaders the Reverend John Robson was unfailingly supportive. Cliff Withey and Lee Maniace were outstanding on the field staff. Raymond Breton and Michael Ornstein, sociologists at the University of Toronto and York University, and psychologist Michael Cowles at York offered constructive advice.

The Eastside project was generously supported by grants from the City of Toronto, the Ontario Ministries of Labour, Education, and Recreation and Culture, the Ontario Economic Council, the Departments of Labour, Health and Welfare, and Manpower and Immigration of Canada, the Atkinson Charitable Foundation, and fifteen corporations and businesses. Notable among the latter were Lever Brothers, Colgate Palmolive, Consumers Gas, Bell Telephone, Manufacturers Life, and Eatons. The Ministry of

Education for Ontario, through a contract with its Research and Evaluation Branch, provided funds for depth interviews in 1979–80 and later analysis of the data.

The co-ordinator and co-author, Harry MacKay, combined commitment to youth with skills as community organizer and researcher. Chapters 2, 3 and 4 are based largely on his master's and doctoral dissertations at York. Marlo Fieldstone and Ron Griffin were outstanding research assistants.

The Social Science Federation of Canada helped with the publication of this book through a generous grant, provided by the Social Sciences and Humanities Research Council of Canada. Readers who wish to aid youth can promote joint ventures by families, schools and employers to smooth the paths toward productive and gratifying adulthood.

*Stewart Crysdale*
*York University*

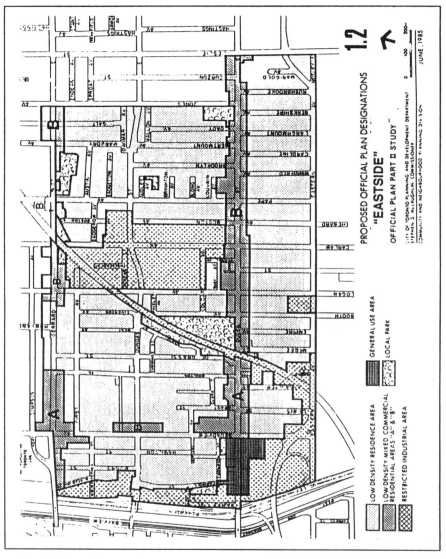

Official plan of "Eastside."

# Abstract

A principal hurdle young people face in industrial societies is the transition from school to work. About two-thirds of youth in "Eastside", a Toronto working class area, leave school without completing any program and commence haphazard, unfulfilling careers. The study proposes that drop-out is partly the result of incongruence in goals and means as between the main socialization agents — family, school and workplace. It also assumes that passage to adult working status is normally developmental, leading from background through early socializing experiences to intermediate outcomes and finally to educational and occupational attainment.

This is a field experiment, comparing a sample of working class youth in downtown "Eastside", who were involved in an intervention program, with a control sample in the same area and a middle class control sample in "Northend" over a twelve-year period, beginning in Grade Eight and continuing into young adulthood. The downtown experimental group of 161 boys and girls and the downtown control group of 152 were interviewed first in 1969 and later during early adolescence and young adulthood. In 1972 the uptown control group of 154 were interviewed, and they were interviewed again in 1974 and 1978. Ninety-nine in-depth interviews were conducted in both areas in 1980, when subjects were in their mid-twenties, and field work continued until 1985.

The intervention program for the DEG included tutoring, supervised and paid work experience one school day a week, assistance in finding part-time and full-time jobs, counselling, a drop-in centre, recreation and cultural outings. The action phase lasted for 28 months.

Certain people were helped to complete school, get better jobs, move smoothly into work and develop higher self-confidence. These were apt to be girls, those from low income homes, youth of British origin (who in this area are less motivated and less inclined toward achievement than non-British), and youth with high intelligence who were dissatisfied with school. At young adulthood the benefits of the program were still felt by some, particularly men, as three of ten in the action group were continuing in education, compared with less than two of ten men in the downtown control group and almost four out of ten men uptown. Downtown young adult women were much less likely than men to return for post-secondary education; uptown young adult women surpassed all other groups in continuing or returning for more education.

The downtown groups during mid-adolescence had economic aspirations and values similar to those of the uptown group, though by late adolescence their real expectations for education and position had fallen much lower.

About four in ten had been tracked into the academic program, compared with six in ten uptown. Tracking had powerful effects of its own on attainment, over and above the effects of intelligence and father's education.

Multiple regression analysis for both areas showed that more education is the chief route to occupational success at the point of entry. Other influential factors are track, early high school performance, educational expectation, and, for youth downtown, self-confidence. Uptown, being a girl and having high job expectation had a positive impact. Individual variables have more effect on mobility uptown than downtown. This suggests that contest is acute among the middle class, while downtown, among working class youth, entrenched structures, particularly in education, suppress individual attainment.

How can we explain the fact that on average, youth in the Downtown Experimental Group who had access to the program did not stay in school much longer than those in the Downtown Control Group who were not included? One reason is the lateness of intervention, not until subjects were already in high school. By the time the program began, many had already dropped out and others planned to do so when they reached the legal school leaving age of 16. Intervention at an earlier age has been an effective deterrent to drop-out in Nordic countries. There all students between Grades Six and Eight are required to take a block of six to ten weeks in career exploration and experience.

Another reason for high attrition in North American low-income areas is youth's demand for money to provide independence and symbols of status, even by means of low starting wages. School tracking into low levels also depresses attainment, as do peer pressure and lack of encouragement by parents and other elders.

Active participation in the project, particularly work experience, helped certain youth go further in school and have a smoother transition to work than most in the downtown control group. This became evident when controls were introduced for the effect of social class, gender, ethnicity, age and intensity of partition in the program.

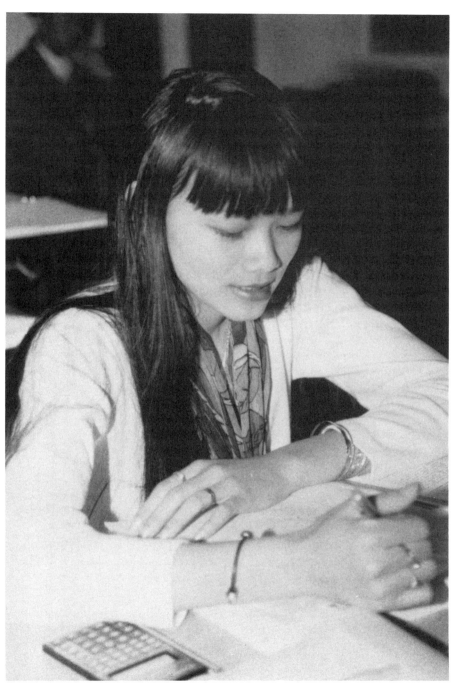
*Eastside—concentration (S. Crysdale).*

*Northend—relaxation (M. Fieldstone).*

# 1

# Youth's Status Passage

The passage of the young from school to work has become a critical social problem for most industrialized countries, including Canada, as they face fierce competition in a technologized world market. Canada's share in this market is shrinking at the same time as its export of raw materials, both eroded by competition from third world nations. This has caused high levels of unemployment among young workers, shortages of skilled workers in some fields and the closing of many manufacturing plants (K. Weiermair, 1986; H. Drost, 1986; L. Marsden, 1986; A. Hassan and P. de Broucker, 1984; OECD, 1984; Canadian Labour Market and Productivity Centre, 1988, 1990). Free trade with the United States has accelerated the problem.

Entrance into full-time employment is a crucial period for individual youth. For most the entry level determines fortunes for the rest of their lives. Starting to work is not a carefree lark. Passage is not stepping happily over a fence that barricades adolescents from earning and handling money, getting married, begetting children, voting and freely entering the beer parlour. It has fateful consequences for future status and lifestyle (Glaser and Strauss, 1971).

For most youth the greatest worry is preparing for and finding suitable employment. In a national survey, Bibby and Posterski (1985:150, 1992) learned that 61 percent of those in their middle to late teens were deeply concerned about careers. When half of Canada's unemployed are under the age of 25 (about 700,000), preparing the young for work has become of paramount importance.

Many heap blame chiefly on schools. The most serious criticism is that the system perpetuates stratification of people into classes, in which the children of the least educated and poorest paid are slotted for low-skilled, low-status jobs, regardless of aptitude or ability (R. Boudon, 1974; R. Breton, 1972; S.A. Bowles and H. Gintis, 1976; Porter, Porter and Blishen,

1973/82; P. Anisef, N. Okihiro and C. James, 1983; S. Lawton and K. Leithwood, 1988).

While the schools must bear a share of responsibility, since they are the most powerful instrument of secondary socialization, the problem is more complex. One underlying problem is discordance in the transitional process between its major agents: families, schools and work establishments. Transition is most successful when the experiences of the young in these settings are consonant and positive. Discordant messages or no clear message at all results in a rough passage for the young.

The process is also affected by social structures and the psycho-social response of the individual. On one side are class differences and variations by ethnic culture, gender, influential models and peer groups. On the other side are value systems. The latter include norms that guide behaviour in particular circles and, at a deeper level, enduring beliefs that result in critical moral choices. Together these factors set priorities in goals and lifestyle that mould individuals' responses to transitional pressures. Beliefs affect self-concept, identity and ambition. These, in turn, are expressed by youth in expectations of their future place in society. Expectations help to determine work habits and school performance and result in benchmark educational and occupational attainments.

In an effort to observe the transitional process from the broad perspective described above, we began in 1968 what turned out to be a seventeen year project. The central focus is on youth in a workers' area we call Eastside, in downtown metropolitan Toronto. It is situated close to the lakeshore, where modest homes crowd into narrow streets and small lots between factories, businesses and warehouses. To compare youth's fortunes in this area with those in the middle class, we selected another area five miles uphill from the busy lakeshore, which we call Northend. There houses are larger and are set in pleasant gardens and quiet neighbourhoods, far from the hubbub of the inner city.[1]

In consultation with local youth, parents, teachers and employers we decided on three purposes for the project. First, it would observe the transitional behaviour of these major actors over a period of several years, forming patterns of growth and development. Second, we would devise, implement and evaluate an intervention program among low-income youth to help them continue in school and build bridges into employment.

---

[1] Life in Eastside is described in the companion volume by Stewart Crysdale, *Families Under Stress* (Toronto: Thompson Educational Publishing Inc., 1991).

Third, to achieve this we would facilitate communication and cooperation between families, educators and employers. This could be done best by community development methods, in which all the actors are partners in the process. A board and operations committee were formed, representing residents and resource people.

## Research Design and Samples

Partly on the basis of a feasibility study in 1968, we devised a field experiment, gathering observations of causal and consequent variables at two times, first, before the intervention program in 1969, and, second, after the program had been in place for over two years, in 1972. The program was made available to one-half of the original sample, being the Downtown Experimental Group, and the other half, the Downtown Control Group, who took the normal course of transition. The two groups were matched by sex, ethnicity, and an eleven-point Mobility Potential Scale. In 1972 also subjects from an external middle-class sample were interviewed in Northend — the Uptown Control Group.

To observe the possible longer-term effects of the program, a third wave of interviews was carried out two years later, during late adolescence, and another wave four years later still, during young adulthood. After two more years, we conducted ninety-nine in-depth interviews with a representative sub-sample of young adults in their middle twenties, enquiring into feelings about transition at each stage. Group and community observations continued until 1985. The worth of qualitative data in throwing light on the selection process has been demonstrated by studies in Australia by R.W. Connell and others in 1982 and in Scotland by A.C. Ryrie and associates in 1981 and 1983.

Two broad assumptions underlie the design; these are based on well tested theories. One is that there is dynamic interplay between the socializing agents — family, school and work establishment; this is often based on partly conflicting goals and procedures. Further, there is tension between individual rights and institutional prerogatives and obligations. Progressive institutions allow for a large measure of freedom and democratic decision-making. But there are limits if goals are to be met. Values serve to establish boundaries and compromises so that contrary interests may both be served in some measure. Values also provide energy and impetus so that individuals may interpret realities and chart courses toward preferred ends (Adams, 1967; Alri, 1980).

Individuals and institutions alike seek to establish consistent patterns of moral or end-serving behaviour. Groups and individuals expect consis-

## Figure 1-1: Stage Model of the Passage of Youth through School into Work

| A | B | C | D | E |
|---|---|---|---|---|
| Background Factors | Other Early Socializing Experiences | Intermediate Outcomes | General Outcomes | Occupational Outcomes |
| Sex* <br> British/non-British* <br> Education of father* <br> Education of mother <br> Occupation of father* <br> Income of family, 1969/72* <br> IQ Score, 1972* | Church attendance, father, 1969 <br> Church attendance, mother, 1969 <br> Church attendance, self, 1972 <br> School performance, 1972* <br> School track, 1974* <br> Influential others, 1972* | Educational aspiration, 1972 <br> Educational expectations, 1972* <br> Job aspirations, 1972 <br> Job expectations, 1972* <br> Self-confidence, 1974* | Educational attainment, 1978* <br> Self-confidence 1978 <br> Beliefs, 1978-80 <br> Ideological/ pragmatic values[+] | Job attainment, 1978* <br> Weekly wage, 1978 <br> Intrinsic/extrinsic job satisfaction, 1978* <br> Regular career lines[+] <br> Upward mobility compared with parents[+] |

* These variables were retained in the final analysis. The others were deleted from the final phase because of weak path coefficients or because they were conterminous with other variables more strongly related with outcomes.

+ These variables are based on 99 in-depth interviews in 1980-81 and are analyzed in Chapter 7.

tency from one another so that predictable and beneficial forms of behaviour may be followed (G.E. Lenski, 1954; E. Erikson, 1963; L. Coser, 1964). When one side perceives inconsistencies or "unfair" conduct on the part of their opposite, trust and goodwill break down. Cooperation, always precarious, gives way to competition and, in extremity, to conflict. This may explode in destructive violence. The recent growth of criminal, gang behaviour in Canada's metropolitan areas, for example, "swarming" in plazas and the spread of drug use, leading to assault and robbery, indicate the breakdown of conventional bonding. More often, however, conflict takes the form of alienation, or a sense of powerlessness and meaninglessness, leading to apathetic withdrawal from dominant, legitimate relationships.

When the path from home and school to work is grossly uneven and youth drop out of school, all parties lose (J. S. Coleman, 1961, 1966, 1974; P. Anisef and associates, 1975, 1980; R. Ferchat, 1986; A.J.C. King and J. Hughes, 1985; H.A. MacKay, 1978; L. Marsden, 1986; Porter, Porter and Blishen, 1982; P. Burman, 1988; G. Lowe and H. Krahn, 1993, 1991; D. Ashton and G. Lowe, 1991). For many deprived youth when adult keepers of power appear to act unfairly, the mandate of a beneficent society is broken.

The second assumption in this study is that maturation is developmental. Peter Blos (1962), R.J. Havighurst (1972), and others established developmental models in stage theories of adolescence. Jean Piaget (1969), Lawrence Kohlberg (1964) and others have demonstrated the developmental nature of cognition and moral judgement. There is much evidence that background factors act on youth to produce intermediate outcomes in the attainment process and these, in turn, lead to what are often irreversible consequences such as inadequate education and dead-end jobs. These assumptions give rise to the main features of the design of the Eastside Project, presented in Figure 1-1.

This model clusters variables in more or less chronological sequence, by stages. The figure includes only those variables which other studies or our observations suggested might be significantly related with intermediate, educational and occupational outcomes. Asterisks in the figure indicate variables which were finally retained in the path models that are discussed in Chapter 6.

The two areas were chosen after inspection of census tract data indicated that they were typical by family income and ethnicity of working and middle-class localities in the metropolis. The downtown area is identical to that chosen by the principal researcher in 1966 for a study of occupational mobility in relation to class, family and community (Crysdale,

### Table 1-1: Interviews by Subsample in Successive Surveys (Percentages of 1969 Numbers Downtown and 1972 Uptown)

|      | Downtown Experimental Group | | Downtown Control Group | | Uptown Control Group | |
|------|-----|-----|-----|-----|-----|-----|
|      | n   | %   | n   | %   | n   | %   |
| 1969 | 161 | 100 | 152 | 100 | *   | *   |
| 1972 | 156 | 97  | 142 | 93  | 154 | 100 |
| 1974 | 122 | 76  | 109 | 72  | 132 | 86  |
| 1978 | 95  | 59  | 83  | 55  | 109 | 78[+] |

* The uptown group was not interviewed in 1969.
+ The proportion re-interviewed in 1978 was larger uptown than downtown because the latter, original sample was involved three years longer than the uptown group and hence was harder to find.

1991). It consists of three census tracts where in 1971 the average total income per household was under $8,000. The uptown area is larger, providing more space for families and bearing the signs of a flourishing middle class. In the three census tracts chosen there at random within one mile of the secondary school, the average total family income in 1971 ranged from $12,000 to $26,000 (Canada Statistics, 1971).

The original downtown sample of 313 boys and girls was chosen systematically from a list of graduates in 1967, 1968 and 1969 from the senior elementary school which serves the area; every other name was chosen. A matched sample of 154 Northend youth was selected in 1972 from a composite secondary school in that area.

Table 1-1 shows the numbers interviewed in each subsample in the four survey years. Because of attrition, the 1978 sample is not identical with the 1972 sample. A comparison of background characteristics for the two years shows that in the 1978 downtown samples, family income had declined since 1972. In the uptown group there was a slight increase in family income. The education of parents in the downtown groups in 1978 was on average lower than in 1972; that of the uptown group did not change. Fathers' occupation downtown declined slightly while the average uptown rose. Hence, the downtown sample we talked with in 1978 were slightly more disadvantaged in comparison with the uptown people than was the case in 1972. Contrasts in outcomes between youth in the two areas normally would be more severe in the later time. As a result, the benefits of the intervention program are not likely to be exaggerated. Moreover, comparisons are valid because we standardize or control for critical background variables.

The timing of the project was fortunate for interesting results because the area experienced radical changes in the 1960s and 1970s. A substantial shift in population occurred. Not only were new Canadians moving into smaller homes in the area and middle class "yuppies" into larger ones. Increasing numbers were moving out, particularly upwardly mobile growing families who chose suburbs further east and north, and also aging old-timers who were no longer able to live on their own. Moreover, during the seventies, full-time employment for women became the norm, contributing to family change and instability.

Most teachers, business people and professionals who now work in the area leave in the afternoon for home and residential roles elsewhere. Voluntary organizations, including Protestant churches, are now poorly attended and for the most part are led by non-residents. Communication and cooperative action between socializing agents are meagre. Few parents are involved in school matters beyond minimal attendance on visitors' nights, and few teachers are acquainted with residents, their interests and problems. Some parents are employed by local firms but cooperation between employers, parents and teachers on behalf of youth is negligible and perfunctory.

In these circumstances it is not surprising that downtown youth often have little knowledge of cultural, educational and employment resources or opportunities. Counselling in schools is widely criticized as understaffed and poorly equipped. These conditions, along with rising expectations and the desire for money to buy prestigious consumer goods and services, contribute to high drop-out rates in the inner city.

In our 1968 feasibility study, we found that 63 percent of youth over the legal school leaving age of 16 years had left school without completing a program. In the winter of 1968, 45 percent of them were unemployed. Educators questioned our figures. But six years later, in a citywide survey of drop-outs, the Board of Education found that 60 percent left school without completing Grade 12 or 13 (Young and Reich, 1974). The rate in low income areas was higher. The overall drop-out rate for the city was two and a half times higher than that for suburban areas. The overall provincial rate of drop-outs has been one-third for over a decade (Ontario Premier's Council, 1988; E. Karp, 1988).

Disjunction between downtown schools and other socializing agents is also illustrated by the tendency to stream students into a terminal rather than the university bound track. The proportion of those in shorter programs is about two-thirds, compared with one-third in middle-class areas (Buttrick, 1977; Wright, 1970, 1972; Dhantoa and Wright, 1980 ). Finally the support given by parents of British origin for obtaining good grades and completing a program is lower when income is small, especially in larger families (Breton, 1972).

## Reasons for Leaving or Staying

Reasons given by downtown youth for not completing a program form a pattern of relative deprivation at home, lack of personal or subject interest at school, failure, and desire for consumer status or financial independence. Five times as many youth of British origin drop out, compared with non-British. Those of French-Canadian origin are also more prone to leave.

> Mac enjoyed his friends at secondary school but found the subjects boring and teachers uninterested in him. While in Grade 10 he got into drugs — marijuana and LSD. "I didn't shoot it. I like poetry and meditation and drugs helped bring body and soul together ... I left for a free school but this didn't help serious studies. I needed money for my habit so went to work ... I'm taking treatment now. I'd still like to be a poet and study religion. Maybe when I get better I'll be a cook."

> Brad left after Grade 10. "Like my dad, I was forced to go to work as we needed the money. Besides, it was nice having cash in my pocket. I operate a machine ... My brother-in-law drives a truck. He also had Grade 10. He makes from $400 to $500 a week and you tell me we need an education?"

> Francine was at her fifth job in four years but liked it and thought she'd stay. "I left after Grade 9 but took typing and bookkeeping at night school. I first worked in a factory but after night school got better jobs ... I'm very satisfied now. What they teach you in school is of little use. Every company has its own ways and they help you get started, like with computers ... I'd definitely have stayed in school if there's been on-the-job training at the same time ... All my friends quit school when I did."

> Then there was Allie, whose parents also were from Europe and didn't speak English well; neither had they gone past the first year in high school. But her dad used to read to her and take her to the library often; she had to read back to him, too. "I would have gone on past Grade 13 but there was no money, so I had to work ... I worked at the racetrack for a while but the pay was poor and hours long. So a friend told me about the bank. I've been there three years and really like it. They pay for me to take night courses at university."

In contrast with the downtown, British-origin youth, who tend to leave school early, very few uptown youth, regardless of ethnicity, do not complete at least Grade Twelve and many go to post-secondary levels. There are some exceptions.

> Donald left during his second year in Grade 11. "I had a learning disability and wasn't smart enough to go on." But later he said that when his parents split up a few years before he entered high school, he went to live with his uncle and they were always short of money. No one tried to talk him into staying at school when he decided to leave. "Now all I can get are rotten jobs, with lots of pressure and low pay. I hate them and the people who run the businesses." He'd rather be a musician.

> Barry missed one subject in Grade 12 and tried to go back. "I couldn't hack it. I had trouble with attending and discipline. It's important for me to work with my hands and I'm in the second year as an apprentice ... auto mechanics ... It's OK ... All my friends went on to university, like my parents did. They never tried to get me to continue ... I liked mother but dad and I never got along." At that point his father confronted the interviewer angrily and shouted, "You have no right to come here without an appointment." Barry is just back from a trip to Europe with his girl friend. He plans to live with her or his brother.

> Steve left Grade 13 during the teachers' strike, but after a series of dirty jobs decided to go to community college and learn a trade. He remembered that a teacher got him interested in art and design and that "turned on a creative urge in me." When he was laid off a temporary job a Manpower counsellor got him into a sponsored program at college. Now he's becoming a boat builder. "Not what I'd dreamed of ... to be an industrial engineer. But I do like it and it's a rewarding job." While not close to his dad, when in high school they talked about careers. "It was very helpful ... They always wanted me to go on but didn't push ... When I got brainwashed by a cult for eight months, the family waited for me to come to myself. They're always there."

> Eleanor's mother is a professor and it never occurred to her not to go to university. All her mother's people had professions. Her dad, who was a skilled tradesman from Europe, left the family when she was in elementary school. Though not close to him, she respects him and sees him regularly. But it was her mother who really raised her and supported her plans. They are very close. "I'm just about through law school ... Peace is my main concern ... If we're honest, including lawyers, and work for freedom for everyone, there will be less fighting and war." She believes her schooling was excellent, thinks it should be stricter, believes in streaming — and capitalism.

## Relevant Studies: Impact on Public Policy

The examples above underline the urgency of family support for the long journey toward a good education and a productive career. But they also carry another message. Many bright and ambitious youth, regardless of family support and regardless of ethnic encouragement or lack of it, have to endure what seems to be a needless struggle to stay in school or return to it after negative experiences in early employment. Many studies in the United States, where Canadian educational policy makers often go for models of change, have found their system to be sadly lacking in meeting the needs of almost half of students. In recent years numerous Canadian studies have pointed toward the need of reform in this country as well. What has been the result?

Generally, policy makers in Canada, as in the United States, have ignored the recommendations of independent researchers for reform, usually based on impeccable research. Paul Anisef and associates (1982), after conducting thorough enquiries into the problems of Ontario students in completing secondary and post-secondary programs, conclude that successive governments continue to assume that only the provision of loans and grants to deserving youth will solve all their woes. Many years of this have not stopped the bleeding. Basic changes at deeper levels in curriculum and real accessibility are required. While shortage of funds prevents many deserving and promising youth from obtaining the appropriate education to contribute to society and to fulfil themselves, an even more fundamental requirement is closer attention to the *variety* of needs to be met in a complex post-industrial age. More responsiveness and flexibility are needed in curricula, teaching methods and administration.

What, then, is the use of more studies such as this one? For one thing, we don't give up on educators and policy makers. While some teachers and bureaucrats are indifferent, others see the need for change in the new times and generation. The problem is not simply *Inertia*. It is inertia grounded on confusion and lack of consensus as to goals and means. Some of us believe that the accumulation of knowledge will in time dispel much of the confusion and erode *Inertia*. Then there is public opinion. In time of uncertainty about the future of the economy and the place of education, there is a tendency to turn to old verities from past experience. But there is also a creative minority — small, as the prophet said, as a tiny cloud in the sky, the size of a human hand in immense space — who are bearers of innovation that may turn a situation around. So researchers and innovators may take heart. Like prophets before their time, they have a job to do.

Most large studies in Canada and the USA have focused on inequality of opportunity. James Coleman's (1966) massive study of the disadvantages of Black students in public education was perfectly timed, coinciding with awakening public consciousness and undergirding a Supreme Court ruling on constitutional rights. It helped to implement new laws raising the standard of education for minorities.

The recommendations of other large American studies have not yet been implemented. But they focus attention on specified action when the time arrives. Project Talent, after 20 years of enquiry, urged that more flexible forms of education be instituted to maximize students' potential (Flanagan, 1978). The eight year study of 2,200 American teenagers, Youth in Transition, concluded that counselling and streaming in high school are too late and too rigid to get results; sensitive shaping must begin in early grades (Bachman, O'Malley and Johnston, 1978). The authors also found that the role of schools in credentializing students for various destinations is counterproductive for effective education. It turns teachers into gods rather than mentors. Bachman corroborated findings of the Panel on Youth of the President's Science Advisory Committee (J.S. Coleman, 1974) that students should be allowed to leave school for work and return later, with greater knowledge and motivation, without suffering failure or other debarment. The National Commission on the Reform of Secondary Education (1973) advised that programs be worked out dually between schools and employers. Most authorities in the USA and Canada have not yet moved in this direction at the secondary level. A few universities and many community colleges in both countries have done so, to the advantage of job entrants and employers (F.N. Heinemann, 1981; R.E. Slavin, 1990; D. Boud, 1985, R.I. Simon, 1991).

Although the cultural and political background of Quebec in some ways sets education there apart from Anglo-Canadian education, their students experience similar problems in transition and employers complain of distance between school and work and acute shortages of qualified young workers in many fields. More than a dozen volumes have been produced by researchers since the early 1970s under the enquiry headed by Pierre W. Belanger and Guy Rocher, "Aspirations Scolaires et Orientations Professionelles des Etudiants." In Volume XI Herbert Horwich (1980) reports on Social and Cultural Factors Affecting Educational Retention and Acquisition at the Secondary and Post-secondary Levels in Quebec. Using factor analysis, he compares the strength of five independent variables in affecting the retention of students into senior high school. While family status, or class, has a strong impact at this stage, it is surpassed handily by educational aspirations, explaining 41 percent of variance. This is followed, in turn, by self-confidence, school performance and, finally, occupational aspirations. Drop-outs from Quebec's secondary schools are weak in all of the above "predictors" of success, leading to the conclusion that reform in the system is urgently needed to improve retention and transition.

A new development in Canada may stimulate overdue change in secondary education to improve response to needs of youth and employers. Cooperative education, or work experience for credit under supervision of the school, is spreading rapidly, especially in larger centres. It became widely available only in the middle seventies, but already, as our field work showed, disenchanted students had heard of it and mentioned it as a welcome reform. With tightening world competition, especially based on intensive use of technology, educators and policy makers are under mounting pressure to develop such programs on a wider basis, both in content and scope. The present report's findings add to the sparse store of knowledge on the subject (cf. Ontario Premier's Council, 1988, 1990).

We build on extensive knowledge of the inequalities of opportunity in present Canadian systems, placing children of low income families consistently behind others with privileged background (Breton, 1972; Hall and McFarlane, 1962; Pike, 1970; and Porter, Porter and Blishen, 1973, 1982). In his large national survey Breton drew attention to the bearing of school tracking on aspirations and upward mobility. Those in non-academic streams, which consist mostly of children with low family income, are discriminated against by the system. We explore this possibility in Eastside.

The crucial importance of education as a prelude for occupational level was established by Blau and Duncan (1967), who pioneered in analysis by path techniques, which we use also in this report. In their Wisconsin studies, Sewell and associates (1969, 1970, 1971) added to this model the influence of significant others, such as parents, teachers and peers. We take these factors into account.

Sid Gilbert (1979) modified the Wisconsin model for the path analysis of aspirations of Ontario Grade Twelve male students. By introducing self-concept of ability and pre-university program of study, and retaining family influence, along with socio-economic status and mental ability, Gilbert greatly increased the explanatory power of the model. In this study, we tried self-confidence and family influence as possible predictors of attainment but they did not prove to be powerful enough to retain in our final models. We were able to go beyond aspirations as an outcome because of the longitudinal data. Gilbert showed that family status has a greater effect on aspirations in the Canadian sample than in the American.

He concludes that the Ontario system seems to be more elitist than American systems.

In a longitudinal study of Ontario Grade Twelve students, Anisef (1975) learned that for the majority, expectations do not predict eventual behaviour. However, consistency, or role crystallization, is strong among students with higher grades, who had encouragement from their fathers, and whose parents had high "expectations" for them. Consistency was more common among girls, among those whose fathers had more education than others, and among those who had high confidence in their ability to graduate from university.

Policy and program have not been widely researched in Canada. In this report we touch on implications for both and will draw on several excellent studies which bear on Canadian educational issues. These include reports by the International Commission on the Development of Education (Faure, 1972), the International Bureau of Education (1973), the Organization for Economic Cooperation and Development (1977), and the National Commission on the Reform of Secondary Education (1973). Unfortunately, these and more recent studies in Europe and the United States are not widely known among Canadian educators and policy makers. (eg. W.T. Grant Foundation, 1988, *The Forgotten Half: Pathways to Success for America's Youth and Young Families*; United States General Accounting Office, 1990, *Training Strategies: Preparing Noncollege Youth for Employment in the U.S. and Foreign Countries*.)

We turn in Chapter 2 to characteristics of the samples during early and middle adolescence and trace early experiences. These lead to intermediate outcomes, discussed in Chapter 3. The fourth chapter deals with changes in aspirations and expectations by late adolescence, and early educational and occupational attainments. The intervention program is described in Chapter 5, along with its impact in late adolescence and young adulthood. Later outcomes are analyzed in Chapter 6 and the effects of ideology in Chapter 7. Chapter 8 concludes with a summary of findings and recommendations for policy and further research.

# 2

# Experiences in Early and Mid-Adolescence

Early adolescence is an exciting and confusing time. You leave childhood behind and with it the protecting and limiting shelter of the parental circle. Not only must you contend with tumultuous surges in sexuality, cognitive ability and moral judgement. You must also cope with people all around you with backgrounds different from yours and learn new roles for changing positions in dizzying circles of peers and acquaintances. You're under pressure from family and school to perform in ways your elders say are fateful for your social status, whatever that means. To a considerable degree, this performance centres in large classes and schools, where competition is fierce and powerful adults make judgements in impersonal and often "irrelevant" ways. How can a fourteen-year-old understand why marks in maths and history are important for your future? Adult roles are dim and distant. Just the same you have dreams about what you will be doing and who you will be. But only a minority have definite goals and plans to achieve them.

One problem with growing up in North America, says Ruth Benedict (1953), is the discontinuity between responsible and non-responsible roles (cf. John Coleman, 1972, 1974). Social structures that never seem to change delay commitment and maturation. Until youth finish school, some at the age of 25, they are subordinate, marginal to mainstream, productive adulthood, hostages to the future. But they are in a rush to become independent, free, with their very own identity. The rush becomes more frenzied as youth move from early through middle to late adolescence (Blos, 1962).

Against this background we will examine youth's assumption of successive positions along the status scale. How do causal factors affect them at each stage? This chapter deals with the maturation process in the early and middle stages. The first includes youth between the ages of 13 and 15, when they are in Grades Seven to Nine, and the second, ages 16 to 18,

## 2 / Experiences in Early and Mid-Adolescence    17

when they normally are in Grades Ten to Twelve. There are two sections, on background features and early socialization experiences.

## Background

Individuals with varied backgrounds come to occupy socio-economic levels established first by parents' position and by gender with its differing roles. These are handed down and enforced through accustomed practices and institutions. Then social status is affected by developed intelligence, which is also the product of background or endowment, and by ethnicity, which consists of sub-cultural norms and structures. As shown in our basic model (Figure 1–1), background features interact with socializing experiences, to develop behavioural responses. These, in turn, facilitate or impede transition.

### *(a) Socio-Economic Status*

In a survey of the extensive literature in the United States on the subject, Christopher Jencks and associates (1972: 139) estimate that socio-economic status (SES) accounts for 10 to 15 percent of the difference in the educational attainment of youth. Although this may seem to be an unimpressive percentage, the relationship is significant in virtually all studies. Daniel Schreiber (1967: 185) found that 70 percent of drop-outs came from families whose total annual income was less than $5,000. And in a longitudinal study by Robert Havighurst (1962) only four percent of boys and no girls from the lowest of four social classes went to college, whereas 80 percent of the children from the highest social class went.

These and other American studies suggest that background or parental socio-economic status (SES) nearly always determines to some extent the attainments of young adults, but it is most important for youth from poor families. In the United States race is a substantial factor in the impact of SES on attainment. Only three percent of our sample are Black but approximately one-half are from minority ethnic groups. We will examine effects of ethnicity on relations between background SES and attainment in a later section of the chapter.

A number of early small-scale Canadian projects indicate that here also there is a persistent relationship between background SES and educational and occupational attainment (Pavalko and Bishop, 1966; Hall and MacFarlane, 1962; Pike, 1970). In a large national survey of career decisions, Breton, McDonald and Richer (1972) found that differences in plans for post-secondary education between youth from high and low class SES were less for those in non-university than in university programs and that among French-speaking students there was no social class difference in the evaluation of chances for success. They also showed that students from social classes did not differ significantly in values concerning work. But if a student had decided on certain goals, then social origin had an effect on whether education was chosen as the route to attain them (148). The inference is that systematic differences in educational attainment according to background SES may be due not to values held by students but rather to the opportunities open to them.

This explanation is supported by a large scale survey of Ontario students conducted by Marion and John Porter and Bernard Blishen (1973: 91). Twice as many bright students from low status families expected to go to work after high school, compared with those having similar mental ability from high status families. The number of highly intelligent students in low income families who are deprived of higher education is very large, being one-half of students, compared with the 15 percent from high status families. It is apparent from these and other studies that the relations between initial SES and educational and occupational aspiration and attainment are positive and complex (P. Anisef, 1975, 1982; R. Pike, 1970, 1980; M. Boyd, J. Goyder, F.E. Jones, H. McRoberts and P.C. Pineo, 1985).

The direct and indirect relations between background and attainment are fateful from an early age. Gold and Douvan (1969: 127) write:

> The damage of a poor environment has already occurred (by Grade 9); the benefits from a good one have already been established. After that point, the role of socio-economic level as a causative agent ... appears to be indirect, operating on achievement partly through the medium of past achievement.

We will leave for later chapters a comparative analysis of the strength of background SES along with other variables in affecting the aspirations and attainments of our sample. In this section we simply describe variations in background and outcomes.

Table 2-1 shows that the status of the downtown sub-samples, indicated by total family income during mid-adolescence, was much lower than that of uptown cohorts. Approximately one-half of the downtown families reported a total income of less than $8,000: 47 percent in the experimental group and 52 percent in the control group. Only one-fifth of the uptown families were in this unfortunate position.

The lower socio-economic status of the downtown sample is also shown by the occupations of parents. While no downtown fathers were professionals, managers, or owners, 55 percent of uptown fathers had reached these levels. The educational achievements of parents also set the

### Table 2-1: Family Income, by Downtown Experimental and Control, and Uptown Control Groups, in Mid-Adolescence (Percentages)

| Level of Family Income | Downtown Experimental | Downtown Control | Uptown Control |
|---|---|---|---|
| $ 4,999 or less | 20 | 28 | 8 |
| $ 5,000 - $ 7,999 | 27 | 25 | 12 |
| $ 8,000 - $ 9,999 | 18 | 13 | 24 |
| $10,000 or more | 35 | 36 | 56[a] |
| No answer | (9) | (11) | (18) |
| Numbers | 113 | 98 | 114 |

[a] DEG + DCG versus UCG, $10,000 per annum or more: $Z = 3.68$, $p < .001$.

two areas apart. Among downtown fathers 25 percent had an education of Grade Eight or less, 45 percent had some high school, 18 percent had completed high school, 12 percent had some post-secondary education, and none had attended university. In contrast, among uptown fathers 22 percent had Grade Eight or less, 16 percent had some secondary education, 29 percent had completed high school, 12 percent had some post-secondary schooling, and 21 percent had finished university. In the downtown area mothers had about the same education as fathers; many of them less. However, in the uptown area, mothers had attained a higher level of education than fathers except at the university level. Whereas mothers tended to graduate from other post-secondary schools, fathers were more apt to graduate from university.

### *(b) Sex Roles*

Sex-typing by agents of socialization begins early and continues throughout the adolescent period (Maccoby and Jacklin, 1974; Mischel, 1970; Richer, 1979; Armstrong and Armstrong, 1990; Duffy, Mandell and Pupo, 1989; Mandell and Crysdale, 1993). It limits opportunities, particularly for girls, in education and training, in access to jobs and promotion, and in rewards in the form of pay, prestige, and power. And it creates in the minds of the young restrictive norms as to suitable positions and roles and of their capacities to perform in them. Hall and McFarlane, (1963: 19) in an early study of a mid-sized Ontario city, observed that girls were more likely to leave school at Grade Ten, while more boys survived to Grade Thirteen, although it took them longer to graduate than girls.

In an unpublished study of the Eastside sample we found that girls in mid-adolescence dropped out of school earlier and in greater numbers than boys, although they had performed equally well in school. The fact that a large proportion of girls in Eastside are streamed into short, commercial, secondary programs may help to account for their higher drop-out rate. After Grade Ten the girls in commercial courses can obtain low-level white-collar jobs such as filing or typing. This is not the case for boys; they must finish longer technical courses in order to get jobs related to their training.

Another reason for the earlier and higher school drop-out rate for downtown girls arises from anticipatory socialization. The homemaker role still has considerable attraction for lower and working-class girls, compared with middle-class cohorts. Moreover, there is a stubborn tendency for girls, especially in low-income areas, to enter "feminine" programs and occupations.

## *(c) Intelligence*

Logically and by many empirical tests, intelligence is related to attainment. As intelligence consists of native ability and response to social, cultural, and emotional stimulation, it plays an important part in how the individual adapts to opportunities for advancement. In their national survey of Canadian youth, Breton and associates (1972: 140) found that mental ability had more influence on college plans than socio-economic origins had. Their study used tests for mental ability that were not class-biased. Kerckhoff (1974: 89), in a study of ambition and attainment among American boys, learned that Intelligence Quotient score was by far the most powerful background variable in explaining educational attainment. But Kerckhoff and other researchers acknowledge that IQ scores, first, are not a measure only of native ability but reflect also the effect of social experience, and, second, their impact on attainment is affected by other variables such as parents' education, encouragement and help. Hence, although we will treat IQ as a background variable, its functions are ambiguous for it represents also the results of early socialization.

To some degree, also, IQ tests are culture-specific. Usually they include questions on paragraph meaning, speed of reading and word discrimination, all of which reflect the elaborated middle-class culture. Children raised in working class homes or minority ethnic families are at a disadvantage in coping with unfamiliar concepts and language and may be expected to get poorer scores than most middle-class children. The result of poor scores is fateful, however, as children who get low scores are tracked into applied secondary programs that lead to low lifelong positions. Moreover, children soon form an estimate of their own ability and this has a critical effect on performance, aspirations and attainment.

In spite of the bias of IQ scores, we include them in analysis because they were used by schools during the Eastside project and undoubtedly affected streaming and attainment.

The downtown sub-samples had lower IQ scores than their uptown cohorts. In tests given in either Grade Eight or Ten, 7 percent of the Downtown Experimental and 5 percent of the Downtown Control Group scored 120+, or A, but 19 percent of the uptown control group scored at this top level. Conversely, 22 percent of all the downtown students scored below average levels, compared with only 5 percent of the Uptown Control Group.

## *(d) Ethnicity*

Many studies have shown that ethnicity strongly affects school performance, aspiration and attainment and early job attainment. Parnes (1970, 1971, 1973) found that native-born Americans were more likely to drop out of school than non-native Americans (53 as against 37 percent of 14- to 24-year-olds). There is a tendency for immigrants to be upwardly mobile after they arrive in Canada. Edward Herberg (1982) found that minority groups far surpass Canadian-born Anglo- and Francophones in educational attainment, especially Chinese, Greeks, Italians, Portuguese and Ukrainians (Richmond and Kalbach, 1980; Reitz, 1980). Jews, Orientals and Asians are most upwardly mobile.

In the downtown samples the non-British minority aspire to higher levels in education and work during early and mid-adolescence than do the British majority. Numbers in our sample are too small to permit more precise analysis; most Orientals and Asians arrived in the Eastside area since our study began in 1968 (See footnote in Appendix A). Because preliminary analysis showed little variation in attainment by specific north-European origin, we felt warranted in grouping them, together with the few non-whites, as non-British.

We see from Table 2–2 that slightly less than one-half of the downtown sample were of non-British origin and a small majority of the uptown sample were non-British. About the same proportions downtown and uptown were born outside Canada (17 and 16 percent). But more of this immigrant group in the downtown area had come to Canada recently than in the uptown area. Of the downtown immigrants, 34 percent had immigrated since 1964, as against 19 percent uptown. We might expect, therefore, that the downtown non-British youth will strongly reflect the upward

### Table 2-2: Father's Ethnicity, for Three Youth Samples, Mid-Adolescence (Percentages)

| Ethnicity | Downtown Experimental | Downtown Control | Uptown Control |
|---|---|---|---|
| British | 55 | 57 | 46 |
| Non-British | 45 | 43 | 54 |
| No Answer | (14) | (19) | (3) |
| Numbers | 108 | 90 | 129 |

DEG + DCG versus UCG British: $Z = 1.74$ $p < .05$.

aspirations of their immigrant parents. Also the uptown non-British families have reached higher status in education, occupation and income than the downtown non-British people partly because of their longer time in Canada. In the downtown sample, 31 percent of the non-British fathers completed Grade Eight or less as compared to 21 percent of the British fathers, and half as many non-British fathers completed Grades Twelve or Thirteen as British fathers, 11 percent and 23 percent. However, as noted, not one British or non-British father in Eastside graduated from university.

In the uptown area, 27 percent of non-British fathers had less than Grade Eight education as compared to only 16 percent of the British fathers. But both British and non-British fathers achieved nearly equal levels of higher education. Twenty percent of the British fathers and 22 percent of the non-British fathers graduated from university.

The educational background of the downtown mothers is similar to that of the fathers. Fifteen percent of the non-British mothers completed some post-secondary training, mostly in nursing, education or business, compared with 10 percent of the British mothers.

In contrast to the downtown group, 22 percent of the uptown British and 11 percent of the non-British mothers graduated from a non-university post-secondary institution. In the uptown area also 12 percent of British mothers and 11 of the non-British mothers graduated from university.

No father in the downtown area held a professional job, from either British or non-British background. However, a larger proportion of downtown non-British fathers, 38 percent, were skilled craftsmen, compared to 30 percent of the British fathers. A similar proportion from each background were on welfare or were disabled, 15 percent of the British and 17 of the non-British.

In contrast, in the uptown sample, 49 percent of the British fathers and 40 percent of the non-British fathers had high level occupations. More non-British held skilled jobs, 29 percent compared with 24 percent of British fathers. Only three percent of the British and four percent of the non-British were on welfare or were disabled.

In summary, then, the non-British fathers in the downtown area on the whole had somewhat less education but held slightly better jobs than the British, though their family income was somewhat lower. Uptown, non-British fathers had more education, better jobs, and higher income than their compatriots downtown but were at a disadvantage in all these respects compared with British uptown neighbours. In the downtown area we will find that their children surpassed youth of British origin in aspirations, expectations, school performance and attainment, in spite of socio-economic disadvantages at home. Other factors must have motivated them to achieve at a high level, particularly values and ambition.

## Early Socialization

Socialization, as noted earlier, is a two-way process. On one side, initiative comes from basic institutions, such as family, education and employment, which exerts pressure on new members to conform to established norms, values and patterns of behaviour. On the other side is the response of the individual through internalization of accumulated knowledge, skills, and values.

To an important degree we become what we see. Modelling, Alex Inkeles (in Clausen, 1968: 121) has said, "implies that children will be influenced not only by being told what they should be like, but by observing what important people in their environment are actually like."

When parents, teachers, and other adults portray desirable behaviour, youth normally select models from among them and fashion their own expectations of future behaviour on their models. "Significant others" also dispense rewards and sanctions for approved values and appropriate actions. The expectations and behaviour of peers also provide standards.

Breton (1972: 384) found that significant others positively affect career decision by youths, while their absence leads to career indecision. The Eastside data show that the influence of significant others is strongest during early adolescence. Eighty-four percent of early adolescents in Grades Seven, Eight and Nine reported that adults influenced their educational and occupational decisions. But three years later the percentage fell to 68 percent for students in Grades Ten and Eleven, and then to 51 percent for those in Grade Twelve (Mackay, 1973: 51).

Socialization variables include closeness to parents, parental pressure concerning future goals, the influence of teachers and peers, and wider association through churches, part-time jobs, ethnic groups and school track.

## *(a) Closeness to Parents*

Extensive research indicates that early relations with parents are the most important factor in determining the kind of person the child will become and how the child will tackle problems on the road to maturity. Rosenberg (1965) found that children from higher social classes are more likely to accept themselves than those from the lower social strata. Further, class differences in self-esteem are considerably greater among boys than among girls (1965: 40–41).

Our data indicate that downtown, chiefly working-class boys had slightly closer relationship with their fathers than did the uptown, chiefly middle-class boys. However, uptown girls reported slightly closer relationships with their fathers than did downtown girls. More girls in general, compared with boys, reported being close to their fathers.

Closeness to mother is of even more importance (Erikson, 1963: 285). In our sample boys were slightly closer than girls to their mothers. For example, a downtown boy who viewed his relationship with his mother as very close stated that "we were very good friends. She treated me as an individual, not as a son." Downtown boys were almost as close as uptown boys to their mothers. Finally, uptown girls were somewhat closer to their mothers than downtown girls.

Louise exemplifies an uptown girl who was extremely close to both her parents. Her father was a role model for decision-making, especially for schooling and career. She is an achievement-oriented university student in Commerce and Finance. Prior to her venture in business she studied to be a lawyer like her father. But the course was unappealing and she dropped it. She states:

> When my parents discovered that I wanted to become a lawyer they encouraged me. I don't know why I wanted to become one. I suppose my father imbued me with motives. His views wore off on me.

Paul is a downtown youth who has nearly completed university. To pay his way he takes tough temporary jobs and moves from boarding house to boarding house. He hopes to find stability and fulfilment by entering the priesthood. He recalls that he was closer to his father, an invalid, than to anyone else.

### Table 2-3: Perceived Positive Parental Influence, by Downtown Early and Mid-Adolescents (Percentages)

| Type of Positive Parental Influence | Perceptions of 13- to 15-Year-Olds | Numbers 231 | | Perceptions of 16- to 18-Year-Olds | Numbers 231 |
|---|---|---|---|---|---|
| *Advice* | | | | | |
| Father | 26 | 201 | | 47* | 207 |
| Mother | 31 | 223 | | 55* | 224 |
| *Pressure for Education* | | | | | |
| Father | 42 | 206 | Father and Mother | 68* | 223 |
| Mother | 58 | 225 | | | |
| *Practical Help* | | | | | |
| Father | 21 | 145 | Father and Mother | 30* | 194 |
| Mother | 21 | 182 | | | |
| *Assessment of Chances for Success* | | | | | |
| Father | 8 | 147 | | 25* | 129 |
| Mother | 14 | 172 | | 30* | 144 |

* Significant at .001 as compared to perceptions when 13 to 15 years old.

During the years my father was a cripple I had a great deal of responsibility to run errands, give him medication. *I absolutely depended on him* until he died, when I was 12. When my father died there was a gnawing vacuum ... From my father I learned that you can go on living, to struggle against all odds.

### *(b) Parental Pressure Concerning Goals*

Parental pressure concerning future goals of children has been widely researched (Kerckhoff 1974: 91; Maizels, 1970: 121). Table 2–3 portrays downtown youths' perceptions of parental influence in early and mid-adolescence. Almost half of the 16- to 18-year-olds reported positive effects from fathers' advice, and over half from mothers' advice. Perceived positive advice by parents increased considerably by mid-adolescence. Downtown youths' perception of parental assessment of their chances for success also increased.

Several things may be happening. Parents were seen in a poorer light by early adolescents but more favourably by mid-adolescents, when they had won more independence and developed some maturity. The poor school performers and the school drop-outs were most apt to report that they had been positively influenced by parents and most encouraged by them to complete school. As the likelihood of poor performance and non-completion persisted, so did perceived parental pressure and encouragement (Mackay, 1973: 52).

Seymour, a downtown youth, is a successful pastry chef. He was in the food processing course, where, however, his marks were poor. In spite of family instability he remembers that his parents gave him considerable support.

> It was difficult to study at home because there was a great deal of noise and quarrelling. There were big fights when my father was drunk. The cops were called ... My folks still encouraged me to study. They said, "You must study if you want to be somebody. If you don't want to study you'll grow up to be a nobody ... " I could discuss with both my parents my school problems.

### *(c) Significant Others: Teachers*

Did the influence of school personnel also change during the teens? Table 2-4 shows a decline over three years in classroom teachers' influence. The perceived positive influence of guidance personnel increased. The classroom teacher's assessment of chances for success increased as well.

While early adolescents thought that teachers were as helpful as parents, only half of mid-adolescents thought that teachers were as helpful. For both early and mid-adolescents, the teacher's assessments of chances for success were similar to their mother's assessments.

The decline in mid-adolescents' perception of the helpfulness of classroom teacher's advice may stem partly from the teacher's role as evaluator. Twenty-five percent of the downtown youth sample failed the first year of secondary school, and quite a number of the sample had dropped out of school by mid-adolescence when the age for voluntary attendance was reached — 16 years. As a large proportion of youth did not fare well in secondary school, some blamed their teachers.

The lowered perception of teachers' helpfulness may also be due to the fact that mid-adolescent have new concerns for full-time work prospects. They see parents as having expertise in the area of work, but not teachers. The decline in teachers' prestige as well may be due to changes in approach. Out of respect for the growing independence of mid-adolescents many give advice only when asked.

## Table 2-4: Perceived Positive Influence of Teachers, by Downtown Early and Mid-Adolescents (Percentages)

| Type of Teacher | Perceptions of 13- to 15-Year-Olds | Numbers 231 | Perception of 16- to 18-Year-Olds | Numbers 231 |
|---|---|---|---|---|
| Classroom Teacher | 32 | 227 | 23* | 226 |
| Guidance Teacher | 17 | 227 | 26* | 226 |
| Classroom Teacher's Assessment of Chances for Success | 20 | 118 | 32* | 104 |

* Changes in positive perceptions between 13 to 15 and 16 to 18 years: Z = from 2.10 to 2.37, $p < .05$.

A downtown girl and graduate in business was an honours student throughout high school. Yet she is bitter towards the educational system and teachers in particular.

> The teachers made me feel that I wanted to leave school yet I didn't leave. Why ruin a perfect honour graduation diploma? They were a pathetic lot. It's not their fault they are ineffectual. They are victims of the bureaucracy. They mean well, but they don't do well, because they are caught in the bureaucracy.

### (d) Peer Groups and Friends

Downtown youth think that the advice of friends is helpful in the same proportions during early and mid-adolescence. About one-third perceived friends as providing helpful advice in both stages.

Thus, parents' perceived helpfulness increases, that of friends remain constant, that of classroom teachers decline somewhat, and guidance teachers helpfulness increases because of presumed knowledge of the world of work.

A different comparative measure of change in the influence of others is given in Table 2-5. The steep overall decline is due to the near disappearance of teachers' influence and the increase in self-reliance expressed in the reply, "no one influenced my decisions." Parents' influence also declined, as did that of friends. Given a choice, four in ten youth by mid-adolescence said that "no one" was influential, this proportion rising from 6 in early adolescence to 42 percent.

### Table 2-5: Changes in Perception of Others as Most Influential, by Downtown Early and Mid-Adolescents (Percentages)

| Type of Significant Others | 13- to 15-Year-Olds | 16- to 18-Year-Olds |
|---|---|---|
| Parents | 50 | 39[a] |
| School | 28 | 7[b] |
| Friends | 13 | 9 |
| Other | 3 | 4 |
| No One | 6 | 42[c] |
|  | $N = 207$ | $N = 226$ |

[a] $Z = 2.35$, $p < .05$, [b] $Z = 5.94$, $p < .001$, [c] $Z = 8.5$, $p < .001$.

Downtown youth accepted the advice of parents almost twice as much compared with school personnel during early-adolescence, and by mid-adolescence, almost six times as much. Mid-adolescents relied increasingly on parents' advice while the influence of friends and school personnel declined. The most prominent aspect of the change in effectual advice, however, was the increase in the proportion who said again they didn't take anyone's advice. This confirms our earlier observation of growing independence through the stages of adolescence. We will return to this theme in Chapter 3 under the section on self-confidence. The influence of family among downtown youth in mid-adolescence, as stated, may be partly a compensatory process. When some students fail in secondary school or drop out, most parents are solicitous and supportive. Poor performers retreat to the homogeneous world of family and a few friends. They are not required to pass; they are accepted just as they are.

### *(e) Secondary Associations*

The range of models with relatively high status is more limited downtown partly because social bonding occurs typically in the narrow circles of family and close friends. Youth who participate in secondary associations have more contact with a variety of possible models. We may hypothesize that the more frequent and varied the secondary socializing experiences, the stronger and broader their impact will be on later status attainment.

The two area groups participated about equally in extra-curricular school activities, less than one-quarter, and in community organizations, 46 and 40 percent. The higher rate for downtown youth no doubt is inflated by the involvement of half the experimental groups in project activities.

Church attendance once a month or more is the variable in which the sub-samples differ most. Twice as many uptown youth attended church regularly, when 16 to 18 years of age, as compared with downtown youth, 26 versus 15 percent. The decline in church-going and diffuse leisure activities by downtown youth as they grow older suggest that social relations are narrowing.

An exception is an uptown boy, a non-British, devout Roman Catholic whose religious interest affects his view of himself and his future. He attends church twice a week because it shapes his thinking and social bonding. "I started going to church last year because I was looking for answers — about life, about religion, something I could build myself on, a sound base, since my old base was not solid."

Sherif and Sherif (1965: 236) wrote that joining a church group generates new aspirations and concerns. Church involvement widens the circle of models for maintaining or striving for high status. Middle class youth more than working class youth tend to take part in adult planned activities.

### *(f) Part-Time Jobs*

Part-time jobs help youth test the "real" adult world (Havighurst, 1962: 131). They meet consumer desires for prestigious symbols of belonging, from records, tapes, compact disks, to clothing, cars and spending money. Part-time work assists in the search for identity through interaction with others in responsible tasks. It is also an early link in a chain of experiences leading toward full-time jobs which are the principal status determinants in our market economy (Keil, Riddell and Green, 1966). Most part-time jobs are dead-end but when they are vocationally relevant they affirm the proximity of adulthood and growing competence to assume adult status and responsibilities (Gold and Douvan, 1969: 258).

Over one-third of downtown students held part-time jobs in the first and/or second year of high school, slightly more than uptown youth. In recent years part-time work among teenagers has escalated to 70 percent (Crysdale, King and Mandell, forthcoming). In Chapter 5 we will find that greater part-time job experience downtown was due to opportunities provided by the Project. In many cases part-time jobs in the project led to full-time careers. This rarely happened among the control groups, whose part-time jobs usually were not related to education.

Since the 70s part-time work has become the sole means of income for rapidly growing numbers, consigning them to marginal status. Roughly three-quarters of upper high school youth are now involved. Many part-timers become so caught up in conspicuous spending that their school performance drops and they frequently give up earlier notions of careers (R.D. D'Amico, 1984; A. Greenberger and L. Steinberger, 1986).

## *(g) School Track*

Tracking, or streaming, is the mechanism many school boards use to sort students from elementary school into secondary programs. The five-year academic program is designed primarily to develop general knowledge and to enhance the ability of "good" students to reason abstractly and critically. It continues in part the tradition of European grammar schools, or gymnasia, which prepared elite students for university. Since the Second World War, school boards greatly expanded other streams for students whose chief interests seemed to lie in technical, commercial, or vocational subjects. Completion of the four-year technical or commercial program could lead to university eventually, but this does not happen often and most graduates from these programs either go to work or enrol in colleges of applied arts and technology. Few enter apprenticeships because of low wages, length of time, and dirty work. Students in two-year vocational programs for the most part have greatest difficulty in transforming education into employable skills and satisfying careers.

Since the project began in 1969, Ontario secondary schools initiated the credit system, which permitted students considerable latitude in selecting courses. Recently, requirements have been tightened again but students are still sorted into basic, general and advanced levels. In effect, tracking functions to provide credentials for either post-secondary education or for employment in the late teens. The sorting occurs in Grade Eight, when students are 13 to 14 years of age.

Tracking at the point of entrance into secondary school has come under considerable criticism in recent years, chiefly on the grounds that it perpetuates class differences in controlling access to university. Another criticism is that students are too young and inexperienced at 14 to understand or demonstrate suitability for one program in preference to another. Reformers argue that the system is too inflexible and provision should be made for students to switch from one program to another without losing a year. The ideological problems of tracking are discussed more fully in the concluding chapter.

## 2 / Experiences in Early and Mid-Adolescence

Our interest here is in the functions of tracking as, first, a sorting device and, second, as a socializing agent. The system sorts students for high or low status futures largely on the basis of presumed ability and academic performance. For the downtown sample the correlation between *academic track* and IQ score is R.40 (significant at the .001 level), while for the uptown sample it is R.47 (Appendices B and C). One possible explanation of the difference is that downtown school administrators place less reliance on IQ as a criterion for advising Grade Eight students as to program. There is also a slightly weaker relation between track and father's education downtown than uptown, R.21 compared with R.28, (significant at .01).

The established practice is to steer most children of the working class into applied programs and most children of the middle class into academic programs. In fact, 45 percent of the downtown and 66 percent of the uptown sample were in the pre-university track. In terms of searching for and fostering the most creative use of potential talent — a nation's richest resource — the practice is questionable, from the viewpoint of fairness or justice and from the viewpoint of long-term productivity and innovation.

An example of tracking working class youth is provided by a downtown girl who was top student in Grade Eight. She wanted to become a physiologist after completing university. Her father had little education and a disability kept him from regular employment. The guidance counsellor recommended that she attend commercial school so as to be sure of a job. Most students accept the counsellor's advice but she did not. She completed a five-year secondary program and enroled at university for her chosen course.

The socialization function of tracking is both structural and psychological. Students with high aspirations and demonstrated abilities are concentrated in advanced courses and those with lower aspirations and abilities are concentrated in other courses. The ethos of advanced courses challenges and encourages achievement more than that of other programs. Students base their efforts on the expectations of parents, teachers and peers as well as on past performance. This pattern is verified in Chapter 6 which deals with attainments during young adulthood.

Chapter 6 provides evidence, through regression analysis, that the impact of early IQ on educational attainment is overshadowed by the impact of track. It is clear that track has a potential of its own for affecting aspiration and later attainment. It is a powerful socializing agent. This is also concluded by Raymond Breton (1972; 24) in his large study. He found that the effect of program of study on aspiration remained when father's occupational status and student's mental ability were controlled.

Authorities use the tracking system to segregate an intellectual elite at an early age and prepare them for more responsible and better rewarded positions. This is one of the most controversial issues of educational policy and administration (Gilbert, 1977; Radwanski, 1987; Ontario Premier's Council, 1990: 37-39). We will return to the pedagogical and policy implications of tracking in the concluding chapter.

*Northend combo at ease (M. Fieldstone).*

*Stewart Crysdale chats with Eastside students (J. Dawson).*

*Northend cartage despatcher (M. Fieldstone).*

# 3
# Intermediate Outcomes

Maturation, we have shown, melds background with socialization experiences in stages to produce more or less predictable outcomes for youth in their middle years, between 16 and 18 years of age. Semi-permanence wraps itself almost imperceptibly around and within half-adults-half-children. Fully grown but denied responsible roles, they are kept in holding patterns by society until it can absorb them into complex and changing strata. Innocence is recently past and wisdom just beginning when the struggle between self- and other- determination reaches a critical pace. Among the successful, in material terms, fantasy and dreams quickly give place to hard-eyed ambition, performance and marks. Social formation actually began away back in pre-school days. But now, with deadly finality, the race for coveted positions reaches eliminating heats. North Americans tend to criticize Japanese schools for robbing childhood of precious growing time. But try as we will, the illusion of carefree youth in North American, a multi-billion dollar promotional industry, cannot gloss over the unforgiving selection process in which teenagers compete for spoils of place.

Johnnie's background downtown imposed severe limitations from the start. His father went only to Grade Four and his mother a few years longer. "We were always hard up; dad worked as a day labourer and mother was a dishwasher. There was a roomer in the basement and a boarder took meals and lived upstairs. We were so crowded I was boarded out three times. The folks said they wanted me to stay in school but they really hoped I'd get a job soon and help pay the bills. I quit in Grade Ten ... My wife took Grade Eleven ... We don't earn much but we manage and we're happy ... Not much chance of more education ... Guess I'm lazy. I'd like to enjoy my work but there's not much to enjoy in menial labour."

On the other hand, Roberta, though also raised in poor and crowded conditions in Eastside, stayed in school through to Grade Twelve and now works as a bank teller. She likes the people at work, the security and pay;

she's taking courses and hopes to be promoted. "One thing that held us together through bad and good times was going to church ... Beliefs are rules you want to live by."

In Northend, Leslea had a hard start as her immigrant father, whom she loved dearly, died when she was very young and she was never close to her mother. But she told them when she was only about six that she wanted to be an artist. An older family friend encouraged her. After Grade 12 she worked for a publisher for a few years before going to Art College part-time. She supports herself, and, though divorced at a young age, is very happy about what she is doing and where she is going.

Ruhl's parents came to Canada from northern Europe when he was in elementary school. As his father went only to Grade Six and his mother not much further, they were anxious that he finish secondary school and go to university or college. Because of problems with English they weren't much help with schooling but the peer ethos in a Northend school kept Ruhl going. The most supportive person in education and choosing a career was their minister. Ruhl has worked with small businesses and is taking college courses leading to promotion.

In this chapter we compare, for Eastside and Northend, intermediate outcomes such as educational and occupational aspirations, actual expectations, secondary school performance and psychometric scores. We will see in later chapters how these middle outcomes, in turn, led to enduring attainments.

## Aspirations for Education and Occupation

A number of basic studies, using multiple regression analysis, have compared the simultaneous effects of several key variables on the formation of aspirations (Sewell, Haller and Ohlendorf, 1970; Woelfel and Haller, 1971; Williams, 1972). Other researchers have found that aspirations among North American youth are now held in common to a large extent regardless of social class; and they suggest that this grows from an egalitarian ideology that pervades youth culture. A few attribute this to the levelling impact of mass media. We may add four other possible explanations. Universal education has extended upwards into secondary levels and post-secondary education is more accessible; populations are concentrated in larger cities where values are widely diffused; geographical and occupational mobility are widespread, accompanied by increasing technology and new kinds of jobs; and, since the Second World War, there has been a general inclination towards meritocracy. The latter is partly a result

### Table 3-1: Educational Aspiration of Downtown and Uptown Youth Samples, by Age (Percentages)

|  | Downtown Youth | | | Uptown Youth | |
|---|---|---|---|---|---|
| *Level of Educational Aspiration* | *13- to 15- Year-Olds* | *16- to 18- Year-Olds* | *19- to 20- Year-Olds* | *16- to 18- Year-Olds* | *19- to 20- Year-Olds* |
| Some High School | 3 | 9 | 8 | 2 | 1 |
| High School | 26 | 30 | 29 | 12 | 17 |
| College | 13 | 16 | 17 | 33 | 14 |
| University | 58 | 45[a] | 47 | 53 | 67[b] |
| No answer |  | (5) | (3) |  |  |
| N = | 231 | 226 | 228 | 132 | 132 |

[a] Decline in aspiration for university graduation for downtown youth between early and mid-adolescence: $Z = 2.74$, $p < .01$.
[b] Increase in aspiration for university graduation for uptown youth between mid- and late adolescence: $Z = 2.4$, $p < .05$.

of the trend towards large-scale bureaucracies which absorb minority and subordinated groups, such as women and youth.

Hence, it is not surprising that there is convergence in aspirations or hopes between our samples of working-class and middle-class youth. Nearly 60 percent of downtown youth, chiefly working class, while in Grades Eight and Nine, would have liked to go to university. This contradicts studies in the United States a few years ago, which concluded that working-class parents held values that discouraged their children from aspiring to high school completion and upward mobility (Hyman, 1966). The "aspiration gap" has narrowed and is due not so much to differences in values between classes as to structural limits in the stratification system (Turner, 1964; Sewell, 1970; Cicourel and Kitsuse, 1963; and several Canadian studies already mentioned, Breton, 1972; Porter, Porter and Bishen, 1982; Anisef, 1982).

From Table 3–1 we see that by the time our sample were 16 to 18 years old, downtown youth had somewhat lower aspirations for education in comparison with the uptown youth. The gap in university aspirations widened during later adolescence, 19 to 20 years, the proportions being 47 percent downtown and 67 percent uptown. The sample had shrunk somewhat since the early teens and, perhaps, especially downtown, we had lost a disproportionate number of potential drop-outs. In addition, reality bore down more heavily on the downtown group as they recognized the limitations imposed by class.

The decline in aspirations for occupations among downtown youth was also pronounced (Table 4–1, next chapter). Between early and mid-adolescence those who wanted to become professionals, managers, or owners fell from 63 to 52 percent. Among uptown youth in mid-adolescence 71 percent wanted to have high level jobs. Downtown youth persisted in the ideal of achievement in the familiar field of education longer than in the unfamiliar field of work. They lowered aspirations from high level jobs to public service, skilled blue collar and clerical positions. But their hopes were still unrealistic for both education and jobs.

## Expectations: The Reality Gap

What were the actual "expectations," when the interviewees were 16 to 18 years of age, in contrast with aspirations? We anticipated that the downtown groups would revise their realistic educational and job expectations downwards. Parnes (1970) found that 16- to 24-year-old males revised educational and job goals to reflect the reality of their situation. In his British study, Roberts (1968: 174) also concluded that young people adjust ambitions to the market.

A sensitive analytical technique is to measure the size of the gap between aspirations and expectations for groups compared over time. The concept of gap highlights the difference between hope and reality. We assume that the larger the gap the greater the consequent cognitive dissonance. The larger the disparity between hope and realistic expectation, the greater will be the sense of alienation for being denied one's dreams. We anticipate that change in levels of aspirations and expectations, that is, size of the gap between them, will have an impact on school completion.

From Table 3–2 we see that the Experimental and Control groups began from almost identical levels of "aspirations" for college or university but their realistic "expectations" changed. During early adolescence the Experimental Group's aspiration level was 70 percent, but their expectation level was 42 percent, a gap of 28 points, similar to the levels and gap of the Downtown Control Group. By mid-adolescence, the Downtown Experimental Group's gap was 16 points, half the size of the Downtown Control Group's gap, 30 points. Because of their involvement in the project, the Experimental Group had become more realistic, suffering less disillusionment, cognitive dissonance, and alienation than the Downtown Control

### Table 3-2: Gap between Educational Aspirations and Expectations for College or University Graduation, for Three Youth Samples (Percentage Points[a])

|  | 13- to 15-Year-Olds | 16- to 18-Year-Olds | 18- to 20-Year-Olds |
|---|---|---|---|
| *Downtown* |  |  |  |
| Experimental Group[1] | 28 | 16[b,c] | 25 |
| Control Group[2] | 29 | 30[d] | 30 |
| *Uptown* |  |  |  |
| Control Group[3] |  | 7 | 16 |

[a] Percentage point difference between aspiration and expectation.
[1] 70 - 42 = 28; 57 - 41 = 16; 63 - 38 = 25.
[2] 72 - 43 = 29; 66 - 36 = 30; 65 - 35 = 30.
[3] _____ ; 86 - 79 = 7; 82 - 66 = 16.
[b] DEG versus DCG (1972): Z = .68, p < .05 (expectations).
[c] DEG versus UCG (1972): Z = 6.06, p < .001 (expectations).
[d] DCG versus UCG (1972): Z = 6.48, p < .001 (expectations).

Group. The gap between hope and reality was smallest for the Uptown Control Group — only seven points during mid-adolescence.

As the time approached for youth to either leave school for work or to continue in post-secondary programs, the contradictions between hopes and perceived reality were still acute, particularly for working class youth in Eastside.

The school performance of mid-adolescents bears a reciprocal relationship with actual, expected achievement (Sewell, Haller and Ohlendorf, 1970; Kerckhoff, 1974; Gilbert, 1979). By then, 79 percent of the uptown sample expected to graduate from a community college or university as compared to 39 percent of the downtown sample. School marks at this time varied similarly. Indeed, 26 percent of the downtown group failed their year with a grade of under 50 percent, compared with only 7 percent of the uptown sample.

## Psychometric Test Scores

How did the two area samples compare at mid-adolescence in youth's feelings about themselves and others in a variety of ways? Using Cattell's

### Table 3-3: High Psychometric Test Scores of Downtown and Uptown Mid-Adolescents (16 to 18 Years Old)* (Percentages)

| Personality Variable | Downtown N 202 | Uptown N 130 |
|---|---|---|
| 1. Warmhearted, outgoing, easy going, participating | 26 | 33 |
| 2. Bright, more intelligent | 40 | 45 |
| 3. Emotionally stable, mature, faces reality, calm, of higher ego strength | 40 | 49 |
| 4. Excitable, impatient, demanding, overacting | 25 | 20 |
| 5. Assertive, competitive, aggressive, stubborn, dominant | 42 | 37 |
| 6. Enthusiastic, heedless, happy-go-lucky | 30 | 32 |
| 7. Conscientious, persistent, moralistic, staid | 24 | 23 |
| 8. Adventurous, "thick-skinned," socially bold | 28 | 34 |
| 9. Tough-minded, rejects illusions | 37 | 42 |
| 10. Zestful, likes group action | 29 | 32 |
| 11. Self-assured, placid, secure, complacent, untroubled | 36 | 44 |
| 12. Self-sufficient, prefers own decisions, resourceful | 33 | 42 |
| 13. Controlled, self-disciplined | 38 | 35 |
| 14. Relaxed, unfrustrated, composed | 29 | 22 |

* Computed from High School Personality Questionnaire, Form A, 1968-69, by the Institute for Personality and Ability Testing. No answers were given by 29 Downtown youth compared with two Uptown youth.

High School Personality Questionnaire, we totalled responses to ten questions for each of fourteen scales to arrive at scores for individuals. Table 3-3 presents high scores. Downtown youth were slightly higher than uptown youth in aggregates on four scales; they were more excitable, assertive, controlled or self-disciplined, and more relaxed. On two scales they were about the same: enthusiasm and conscientiousness. On the remaining eight scales they scored a little lower than their uptown cohorts: warmheartedness, measured intelligence, emotional stability, adventurousness, tough mindedness, zestfulness, self-assuredness, and self-sufficiency.

The slightly lower scores in the latter categories are not surprising in view of the relative deprivation of a substantial number of young people in the working class area.

We checked zero order correlations between each of the personality scales and outcomes such as school performance, school completion, early full-time job level and problems in transition into work. Only one scale, self-assuredness (self-confidence), was significantly related with these outcomes and the coefficients were not high.

We may conclude that in spite of their disadvantages, most downtown youth, as they matured, were able to adapt psychologically to the limitations of school and work. A sizeable minority, however, could not cope and their situation presents an urgent problem for society.

## Ethnicity and Intermediate Outcomes

The aspirations of downtown non-British youth for university on the whole were stronger than those of the British group. Actual expectations fell in both groups but the drop was less for the non-British. Twenty-nine percent of them, compared with 14 percent of the British, believed they would graduate.

Origin did not make any difference in job aspirations. In realistic expectation, however, twice as many of the non-British believed that they actually would get high positions, 39 as against 20 percent. This reflects their stronger ambition, self-discipline and drive.

Uptown, while most minority youth hoped for high positions, they were "out-hoped" by their better-off, British neighbours. However, in actual expectations the non-British, like their compatriots downtown, pulled slightly ahead.

In school marks, downtown minority youth outperformed the majority, 30 percent of them getting an average of 70 percent or higher in 1972, compared with only 17 percent of the British. The failure rate was high for both groups though less for the non-British. Uptown, however, the British group excelled, 40 percent getting an average of 70 percent or better, compared with 33 percent of the non-British. Those with failing grades came to 6 percent of the British and 9 percent of the non-British.

The effect of ethnicity on school completion was similar in direction. Downtown it was the non-British who tended more to complete a program. Uptown, longer residence in Canada and higher SES level of the British permitted a slightly higher proportion to complete a program.

In summary, downtown youth, already by mid-adolescence, were markedly disadvantaged in educational and job aspirations and expectations, in school marks and in completion. High achievers among them included disproportionately large numbers of immigrants or children of immigrants, in spite of unpromising socio-economic origins.

Among those who disappeared from the action group downtown during the middle adolescent years was Eugene, a Scottish-born lad. When he was 14, his father died, his mother married again and he and his step-father were always at odds. He left home, stayed with friends, went to a foster home and, finally, was taken back to the old country by his grandparents, who wanted him. Eugene had been a fair student and had high hopes of becoming a tradesman, as his father had been. When things fell apart, he tried drinking and a little grass, but the rebel life didn't really appeal to him. He hung around the drop-in centre and workers did what they could for him. It wasn't enough, as his handsome, unhappy face showed. His was a classic case of unfulfilled youth at mid-adolescence.

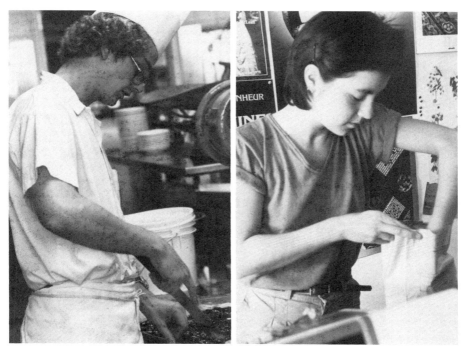

*On their own and loving it.*

*Left: Pastry chef hopes to open his own shop.*
*Right: Proprietor of health food store got her start with parents' help.*
*(M. Fieldstone)*

*Comfortable semi-dense housing in Eastside makes close neighbours of many ethnic groups (S. Crysdale).*

*For some students, bookkeeping comes naturally (S. Crysdale).*

# 4

# Late Adolescence

The previous chapter described the melding of background and socialization during mid-adolescence to produce intermediate outcomes. These affect very strongly the impending passage into employed adulthood. With late adolescence the future comes into sharper focus. At 19 and 20 years, most youth work assiduously at forging an identity. This is a time for consolidation of the elements that determine a destiny. For the minority who continue in post-secondary education, full or part-time, the social destination, with its appurtenances and limitations, is deferred, but only to some extent and for a few years.

The chapter has two sections. The first deals with educational attainment at late adolescence and discusses the suitability of tracking or streaming as a criterion for predicting school success and accessibility to post-secondary education. The other section is on occupational entry, in which we compare job and wage levels for the two class areas during the early years of full-time work, enquire into the shape and length of unemployment, and examine changes in self-confidence. The latter is expected to contribute positively towards mobility.

## Educational Attainment

### (a) School Completion and Drop-Out Rates

By late adolescence the majority downtown had either completed or dropped out of secondary school and attained their highest grade. Table 4-1 shows that 61 percent of the Downtown Experimental Group and 63 percent of the Downtown Control Group had dropped out of secondary school, compared to 32 percent of Uptown Control cohorts. If school and work are portions of the same pathway toward attainment, then the future closes in on most downtown youth before they reach their twentieth birthday. Education for most downtown youth was not a means for upward mobility. But for a sizeable minority it was. Why did some turn schooling to their advantage while others did not or could not?

### Table 4-1: Educational Attainment of Out-of-School, Late Adolescent Samples (Percentages)

| School Attainments | Downtown | | Uptown |
|---|---|---|---|
| | *Experimental* | *Control* | |
| *School Completion* | | | |
| Dropped Out | 61 | 63 | 32[a] |
| Finished High School | 39 | 37[b] | 68 |
| *Last Grade Completed* | | | |
| Grade 8 or 9 | 20 | 25 | 0 |
| Grade 10 or 11 | 36 | 32 | 19 |
| Grade 12 or 13 | 39 | 39 | 67 |
| 1st or 2nd Year College/University | 6 | 5 | 14 |
| | *N = 104* | *N = 89* | *N = 108* |

[a] DEG + DCG versus UCG: $Z = 4.9$ $p < .001$.
[b] DEG versus DCG: $Z = 1.83$, $p$ (approaching significance at .05).

Tom is an example of those who tried against odds to continue in school but finally dropped out — a downtown youth of eastern European background. His father was committed to a mental institution during his childhood. His mother worked in a low status job. Both had very little education. He failed Grade Nine twice, once in the general stream and again in the technical program. He failed Grade Ten due to emotional problems. He went back to school and nearly completed Grade Eleven, but dropped out to work full-time as a cab driver. In young adulthood he is a truck driver. Tom says that failure in school was due to lack of support and guidance from his parents and to emotional pressures at home. Intense quarrelling and frequent beatings hampered his school work.

> I went back to school four years later and went to Grade Eleven. I also worked as a cabby five hours per day. I had to support myself as I lived on my own. The guidance teachers kept hassling me why I came back. I always wanted to be a cop but because of not having the high school minimum and because of a theft problem, I didn't make it. It all became too much — working, studying, the teachers' strike, cancelled classes ... I decided not to go back ...
>
> I don't want anyone's handout. I always felt that people thought that I didn't accomplish anything on my own. I got to prove to everyone that I

## Table 4-2: Reasons for Completing or Leaving School, by Downtown and Uptown Late Adololescents*
(Percentages)

| Reasons | Downtown | Uptown |
|---|---|---|
| *Why Some Completed a Program* | | |
| Education for Job | 62 | 69 |
| Enjoyed School | 27 | 22 |
| Parental Guidance | 12 | 9 |
| | N = 113 | N = 88 |
| *Why Others Dropped Out* | | |
| Dissatisfied with school | 50 | 39 |
| Bored with School | 29 | 36 |
| To Earn Money/Get Married | 20 | 26 |
| | N = 113 | N = 31 |

*Downtown vs. Uptown. Z = 1.15, p < .05.

can get along on my own. I have to be different from my father. But I don't know what I want to do yet.

Table 4-2 shows that students of the downtown and uptown samples who completed secondary school gave similar first reasons. Approximately two-thirds stated that "getting a good job" was the most important reason. But more downtown youth who had left school gave as the first reason for not completing school, dissatisfaction with their school, compared with uptown cohorts. Among uptown drop-outs slightly more were bored with school or left to earn money or to get married.

In contrast with Tom downtown, who left in Grade Ten and was unsuccessful in attempting to continue, Pasquale, whose parents lived uptown, left Grade Twelve short six credits but returned later to pick them up and go on to community college. He hadn't done well in Grade Eight, refusing to study and making a nuisance of himself. His teachers labelled him a slow learner and recommended that he go to trade school. His parents agreed and that's what he did for three years. He hated it and knew that he should be at a higher level. He finally quit, as most of his classmates were doing. He wanted to earn money, follow the crowd.

His was a close family, and though his mother and older brothers and sisters urged him to finish school, his dad didn't insist.

## Table 4-3: Factor Matrix of School Variables for Downtown Mid-Adolescents

| School Variables | Factor 1<br>High School Performance | Factor 2<br>Track |
|---|---|---|
| Grade 9 Average Mark (of oldest sub-sample) | .82 | .21 |
| Last Grade Average Mark | .75 | .10 |
| Last Grade Completed | .74 | .44 |
| High School Program Completed | .70 | .09 |
| Teacher Relationship | .44 | .05 |
| Extra-Curricular Activities in Last Year | .38 | .29 |
| IQ, Late High School | .09 | .61 |
| Grades 7-8 Average Marks (of younger sub-samples) | .09 | .35 |

He left it up to me. I got sales jobs which let me buy clothes at a discount and I could live with my brother; but I knew it was all a mistake ... I really like my dad. He didn't finish high school but later in life he went to university and got a B.A. Now he owns his own insurance company. I respect him. So a few years ago I went to community college and will finish an insurance course next year ... When I was younger, I didn't know what school was all about ... I work part-time to pay my tuition but live free at home, since going back ...

The biggest trouble at secondary school was the discipline. It was a joke ... When I asked Dad about the insurance business, he said, 'Great! I'll help you.' He got information from the college. The rest was up to me.

Beside the gulf in status between the two fathers, they treated their sons very differently. While both were devoutly religious, Tom's dad was brutally authoritarian; Pasquale's was non-directive but loving and supportive. While both patterns are found in the two areas, low status commonly results in restricted opportunities and authoritarian decision-making.

### *(b) The Fallacy of Tracking*

School completion and drop-out may be understood best when we examine them in relation to other school variables. Factor analysis of eight school-related variables for the downtown sample yields interesting findings concerning school performance and school track. Table 4–3 shows the results of Principal Component Factor Analysis with varimax rotation. The high loadings of the first four variables on Factor 1 indicate the chief components of "school performance." These variables include Grade Nine Average Mark, Last Grade Average Mark, Last Grade Completed, and High School Program Completed. The remaining variables — teacher relationship, extra-curricular activities in their last high school year, IQ Score in High School and Average Marks in Grades Seven and Eight, are not strongly related with high school performance. Instead, only IQ score late in high school is related strongly to school track. This means that students in the academic stream have learned to deal effectively with the tests.

Two striking observations follow. One proceeds from the fact that, for the downtown youth, high school IQ score and Grade Seven and Eight average marks are not strongly related with high school performance. This raises grave doubts about the validity of early IQ score and elementary school grades as predictors of success in secondary school.

The other consequence follows from the fact that school track is only weakly related with secondary school success shown by last average mark and high school completion. This casts serious doubt about the stereotype that school counsellors, other education personnel, and the public generally hold of the academic program as being superior in itself for the preparation of students for post-secondary education.

We are led by these findings to question traditional notions about the functions of IQ scores, elementary grades, and tracking which for many years have influenced the policies and practices of school administrations. Tracking favours above average students but handicaps the large majority. Even high achievers are handicapped in transition to work by the absence of opportunities, while at school, to apply and test knowledge and aptitudes. Moreover, the quality of instruction, for example, in maths and science, according to some studies, may be inferior in "low track" schools. Over-all, "inflexible tracking systems perpetuate inequality of opportunity, along with lower average achievement" (Adam Gamoran, 1992).

## Occupational Entry

The downward spiral in aspirations for education as youth enter late adolescence in the downtown, working class area, which we discussed in the previous chapter (Table 3–1), applies also as they leave school behind and enter the labour force full-time.

### Table 4-4: Differences in the Work Characteristics of 18- to 20-Year-Old Full-Time Workers, Downtown and Uptown (Percentages)

| Work Variables | Downtown | Uptown |
| --- | --- | --- |
| *Years of Full-Time Work* | | |
| Less than 6 months | 20 | 39 |
| 6 - 12 months | 20 | 19 |
| 13 - 23 months | 23 | 26 |
| 2 - 3 years | 23[a] | 15 |
| More than 3 years | 15[a] | 2 |
| | $N = 169$ | $N = 65$ |
| *Last Job Level* | | |
| Unskilled or Semi-Skilled Blue Collar | 45[b] | 19 |
| Lower White Collar | 35[c] | 46 |
| Skilled Blue, White, or Professional | 20[d] | 36 |
| | $N = 153$ | $N = 59$ |
| *Wage Level* | | |
| $ 89 or less | 15 | 6 |
| $ 90 - 129 | 41 | 50 |
| $130 - 169 | 32 | 34 |
| $170 or more | 13[e] | 11 |
| | $N = 149$ | $N = 54$ |

[a] $p < .01$, [b] $p < .001$, [c,d,e] $p < .05$.

### (a) Early Job and Wage Levels

Table 4–4 presents very different profiles of the early work experiences of the 18- to 20-year-olds in the two areas. Downtown youth had been in the work force longer than uptown cohorts, twice as many having worked for two or more years. In spite of longer employment, downtown youth were much less represented at the skilled blue collar, white collar, or professional level than their uptown counterparts. Further, Eastside youth on average were earning about the same as their uptown cohorts in spite of longer employment.

Martin is an example of an uptown youth with good job prospects. He had some community college credits and owned and operated his own recording and consulting business for the past five years. His earnings were over $200 a week (relatively high at the time of the survey). He planned to go to university shortly to study architecture. Another innovator is Oliver, a high school graduate. He had been a traffic manager in the past six months at a salary of over $200 per week. He plans eventually to go into his own renovations business. At present he is extremely satisfied with his work.

Typical of most downtown youth, Emil was a high school drop-out. He had been working as a sales clerk for a year at a salary of about $200 per week. He was bored and under constant pressure. He was extremely dissatisfied and was looking for a new position. Another downtown youth, Paul, had nearly completed a university degree in philosophy. He was working as a desk clerk in a men's hostel, earning less than $120 a week. He planned to enter the priesthood, which helped him stand the odium of keeping track of and cleaning up after transients.

Downtown youth did not gain an advantage, even in the short run, by starting work sooner than uptown youth. The two-thirds who had dropped out without completing a program were seriously disadvantaged in many ways, as shown in the following comparisons.

(1) One-third of downtown workers were fired from or quit their last job, with no other job to go to — twice the number of uptown workers. This followed partly from lower quality jobs.
(2) Downtown workers spent more time looking for jobs.
(3) They held unskilled or semi-skilled first jobs slightly more than uptown workers — eight out of ten, compared with seven out of ten.
(4) More downtown workers had negative feelings about their present job, compared to one year previously, than did uptown workers – 19 to 4 percent.
(5) More downtown youth reported having received unemployment insurance benefits — 30 versus 19 percent.
(6) More had no job training of any kind — 40 percent, compared with 10 percent of uptown working youth.
(7) They were more worried about not having enough education — 57 percent compared with 37 percent.
(8) Those worried about knowing how to look for a job numbered 58 percent downtown and 45 percent uptown.

(9) Those worried about not getting a job that they were educated for came to 53 percent downtown and 36 percent uptown.

## *(b) Unemployment*

Among downtown full-time workers, nearly 80 percent found their present job in less than a month, indicating strong initiative and a good labour market. Fifteen percent were unemployed when interviewed, of whom over half had been out of work and looking for at least a month. About one-third had received unemployment benefits at some time. Very few uptown workers had been unemployed or drew unemployment "pay".

After two or three years in the work force, Eastside older adolescents had little job security. About one-quarter improved in job level but 9 percent slipped down and 63 percent reported no change in mobility. The large majority had discouraging experiences, with little or no prospect of steady and promising careers.

Johnnie, who, we remember, dropped out in Grade Ten, is a classic example of downtown youth who end up in a series of unskilled, unsatisfying jobs. Neither of his parents had completed grade school. His father was a labourer. For the past three years Johnnie had operated a paint mixing machine. Before that he had a series of low-skilled jobs and one as a retail salesman which paid very little money. When asked, "Which characteristic of any job would you rate as the most important?" he replied:

> Do I have to pick one? Most everyone would probably choose money. Anyone can pick that. I am miserable at my job, but the money is good and this is very important to me. There is no one to talk to and the work is dull. If it weren't for the money, I'd be out of there in a minute.

Johnnie bitterly sums up the reasons for low aspirations and unsatisfying work situation:

> I never had any real career plans. My parents didn't have any special views towards my jobs. Mother washed dishes all her life; and father shovelled cement in the box cars ... Now I mix paint all day.

## *(c) Changes in Self-Confidence*

In mid-adolescence downtowners were somewhat less confident than cohorts uptown (Table 4–5). By late adolescence, twice as many downtown youth had high self-confidence, almost overtaking uptown cohorts. Neighbourhood in itself did not have a consistent effect on self-confidence. The mere fact that all the sample had matured by two or more years led to gains for most subjects. School success, however, did make a difference. Those who had finished a program or were still studying became more self-confident than drop-outs, one-half versus one-third.

### Table 4-5: Self-Confidence at Two Stages of Adolescence, Downtown and Uptown Samples* (Percentages)

| Self-Confidence Level | | Downtown | Uptown |
|---|---|---|---|
| Mid-Adolescence | Low | 24 | 15 |
| | Average | 40 | 41 |
| | High | 36 | 44 |
| | | N = 190 | N = 130 |
| Late Adolescence | Low | 8 | 4 |
| | Average | 32 | 32 |
| | High | 60 | 64 |
| | | N = 224 | N = 127 |

* Based on Psychometric Test Scores, Cattell's High School Personality Questionnaire.
Downtown vs. Uptown: Z = 1.89, approaching significance at .05.

More boys in Eastside gained in self-confidence, 42 percent as against 36 percent of girls. The intervention program helped, 43 percent of the action group gaining, compared with 34 percent of the control people. Ethnicity made the biggest difference, 52 percent of non-British becoming more assured, as against 33 percent of the British. Peter Blos (1962) observed that youth between 18 and 20 years make strides in consolidating psychic gains and drawing on experience to strengthen identity.

In the Eastside sample, many non-British youth were extremely independent. Asked if her people had helped her make decisions about education and career, Siu-mae, a Chinese-Canadian girl, replied:

> No, they didn't guide me, I have an older sister. She is a comrade. I went to her in the beginning, up to the age of 18, for guidance. Now I make my own decisions ... I had a fear of overdependence on my family. Chinese children do everything for the family; you subordinate yourself. Parents use guilt to achieve this. Father stated that I owed him gratitude for providing for us and working hard for us. Now I am my own self.

Diametrically opposite to Siu-mae in family relations is Jess, of English-Irish descent, born in Eastside, the third of seven children. He left school after Grade Eight because he was suspended for truancy and couldn't catch up. He drifted from job to job until his father got him into the place where he worked. He's always been close to his father and, partly not to disappoint him, never misses work or is late. He's been there seven years and is well paid as a semi-skilled operator. Without hesitation he names "Dad" as the one most helpful in his work. He tries to help others, especially kids who get in trouble. Recently he helped raise money to bury an old friend who died from an overdose; he donated his own cemetery plot. As a young teenager, Jess was a rebel, but now closely conforms to the values of his family.

But family cohesion by late adolescence generally makes little difference in measures of positive transition. In both areas and regardless of gender and ethnicity there is not a strong systematic relationship between "closeness to parents" and attainment in education and work. One reason is that the concept of closeness is too complex for simple analysis. It does appear that those who were close to parents in terms of affection and trust are happier and more sociable. But apart from closeness, if parents support and encourage attainment and this is reinforced by support and direction at the school, youth have a smoother passage into work. We turn in the next chapter to the description and assessment of the Eastside Youth Project, which tried to integrate efforts of family, school and employers to bring about a smoother transition to work.

*Business knows no ethnic boundaries; students in this class came from nine ethnic origins (S. Crysdale).*

*Teachers are intrigued with the companion volume,* Families under Stress *(S. Crysdale).*

*Using the "computerized" printing press (S. Crysdale).*

*Simple hand/mind skills are still basic (S. Crysdale).*

# 5
# The Intervention Programs

The Eastside project in the late 1960s and 1970s provided clear evidence of the need for changes to improve transition. Growing concern over the high drop-out and unemployment rates for young people since the late 1970s led ministries of education and boards of education to introduce a variety of courses to ease transition to work. The most common is cooperative education, in which students, usually in Grade Twelve, may earn credits in school time while getting work experience, under the joint supervision of schools and employers (Canadian Education Association, 1983; Ontario Teachers' Federation, 1983; J. Hughes and A.J.C. King, 1982; A.J.C. King and J. Hughes, 1985; Peel Board of Education, 1987).

While these programs generally have been found satisfactory, little research has been done on the type of students helped, program item effectiveness and long-term results. Further, most studies do not control for the effects of other possible causal variables, such as track, socio-economic status, gender and ethnicity.

The Eastside Project is a prototype for building and elevating such programs, using controls for possible antecedents and following a panel of the same students over a period from early adolescence to young adulthood.

## Development and Participation

Features of the program have been described in Chapter 1. The unusual response of youth, parents, educators and employers over the years is largely the result of a principle built into the project from the start. The community development approach was faithfully followed, in which representatives were involved in the design, implementation and evaluation at every stage. The coordinator and research director spent a year consulting those concerned, forming a representative, governing board, defining objectives and procedures, estimating a budget, and arranging for an operations committee to administer the program. They met once a month for the first three years and then occasionally through to the end of quantifiable data collection in 1980.

A variety of programs were instituted during the first two years. When tutoring sessions were offered first at a local centre only a handful appeared. Then a home program was set up, staffed by volunteer university students who visited and worked with youth once a week at home for as long as there was need and effort. This continued for two years.

A centre was operated in a house trailer on a city-owned corner lot in Eastside for 28 months. It was staffed by the coordinator, a full-time youth worker, a part-time worker, and twenty volunteers. Records, television, pop machine, games, magazines and a lively, accepting atmosphere attracted a core of regular and many occasional members.

Staff personnel called on each action youth at home once a month to discuss school, part-time work and related matters; parents were included. Monthly reports from three of the four secondary schools attended by members recorded attendance, attitudes, and performance.

Monthly tours were arranged to stimulating places and events, including industries and cultural centres; very few Eastside youth had visited such places. Team sports were organized in cooperation with local groups; some games were with suburban youth.

A student employment program was conducted in cooperation with several employers and the Board of Education, whereby, in mid-adolescence, students were released from school one day a week for paid employment related to their school program. The purposes of this program were the provision of needed funds and learning experience outside of but parallel to school programs. Extensive linkages in many European countries between education and employment furnished precedents. A survey of students 16 years of age and older in the Experimental Group showed that over half were eager to take part, and enquiries among employers indicated plenty of openings. A condition was that they pay regular wages and provide supervision and monthly reports

The next step was to get cooperation from the schools and permission from the Board of Education. This took persuasion and time. The plan was set up with youth and employers in the fall of 1970 and presented early in January, 1971 to the Board's advisory vocational committee. There it was supported by the representatives of large employers and one principal but questioned by union representatives and technical and vocational school officials. The latter were concerned that academic standards would suffer and that it would be difficult to adjust schedules in applied courses. Another problem was that the province at that time would not allow credits for work experience. The director of education, however, was supportive, and a number of trustees, especially from downtown districts, were in favour. A few weeks later the proposal passed the committee and finally the Board, which then asked the principals of four secondary schools serving the area to cooperate. In autumn of 1971, 33 students entered the program, the majority from the one school whose principal backed the proposal fully.

The criteria for participation were that students should have at least passing grades but were potential drop-outs. It was expected that the risk of decline in grades due to absence from school one day a week would be offset by improvements in attitude toward work and self. Hence, participants were apt to be grade repeaters, in short courses, from families with low income, having parents with little education, and having low to average IQ scores.

Another program was "Youth Tutoring Youth." Backed by federal funds, this effort employed 14 members of the Experimental Group, who were potential drop-outs, for two evenings a week to help younger students in their hardest subjects. Eleven tutors reported that their own self-confidence increased. Most were from the high school whose principal and staff fully supported the project. Their guidance counsellor observed that all of them improved their own grades and most attended classes more regularly.

The children who were tutored also benefitted. Nine of the 18 class teachers noted an accelerated improvement in skills during the tutoring. Seven of 16 teacher assessments noted a positive change in the children's attitudes toward the subject, work habits and general behaviour. Stanford Achievement Test scores confirmed the evaluations. Not all teachers recognized the worth of the program. The tutor of a Grade Three pupil reported a positive change in both subject skill and attitude over a six month period. The classroom teacher, however, reported no change in either respect. But test scores showed gains of 10 months in understanding word meaning, 13 months in paragraph meaning, and 3 months in arithmetical computation.

The project as a whole had a mixed reception among educators. The director and one of the superintendents were enthusiastic and the Board several times endorsed specific programs, for example, the Student Employment program. But only one of the principals of the four secondary schools attended by members gave consistent support. Some counsellors and teachers took an interest and others did not. A few set tests when students were absent, on permission, for the one day a week employment experience, and refused to reset the tests or permit the students to make up for the day missed.

Eighty-eight percent of the Experimental Group took part in at least one activity. This is high in view of the fact that one-third of the group had turned 16 soon after the first interviews. Half of this older group had dropped out of school before the action programs began. The programs were too late for them.

Intensity of participation was coded as very active, somewhat active, inactive, and non-participating. Very active meant involvement for more than one year. Those most active rated job programs as most helpful while others put peer activities first. Over half of the mid-adolescents in the Experimental Group were somewhat or very active.

## Results in Mid-Adolescence

### (a) Tutoring

Eighty percent of tutored youth improved their grades in the tutored subjects. Youth who sought tutoring were from families with higher than average income and were non-British. They were intelligent and had older siblings who completed school, but their fathers were in lower status jobs. They were also apt to be girls, who, as we have seen, were more likely than boys downtown to drop out of school. They had higher than average educational and job expectations, and higher super-ego strength; they were more conscientious, persistent and moralistic than most (MacKay, 1973: 77–78).

### (b) Part-Time Jobs

The opportunity for part-time jobs and similar early work experience was rated by participants as the most valuable. Over one-quarter said that their part-time work was related to their school courses, as against 9 percent in the Downtown Control Group. The consequences of this connection are discussed in the next section.

### (c) Aspirations and Reality

The impact of the program on aspirations among the action group was discussed in Chapter 3 (Table 3–2). Their grasp of reality in terms of restricted opportunity for higher education and better jobs increased dramatically between Grades Nine and Eleven. It prepared them for more realistic planning and a smoother transition to work at whatever level, although many whose prospects were dim still clung to hopes of high job levels.

## Results in Late Adolescence

### *(a) School Completion*

The proportion of the two downtown groups who completed at least Grade Twelve by the age of 18 years was virtually the same. But comparison is obscured by the fact that one-half of the oldest third left school before the program began. Further, the action group included half who participated very little or not at all. For them the damage of deprivation in home and environment had been done by the time they entered Grade Nine.

The project attracted the participation of action group youth whose home situations were either at the bottom or near the top of the scale; those who were just getting by, with median incomes, did not respond. Among those in the action group who had high intelligence scores, 57 percent completed high school, compared with 47 percent of those with similar scores in the Downtown Control Group. The association between intensity of participation and school completion was strong and consistent for girls. It ranged from 30 percent for girls who, though selected for the Experimental Group, did not take part at all, to 48 percent of those who were somewhat involved, and 53 percent of girls who were most active. In the Experimental Group girls caught up with boys in completion rates, while in the Downtown Control Group they fell far behind.

Similarly, the project helped British-origin youth downtown to stay in school to completion. Among Britons who were active in the project, 47 percent completed school or were still studying, compared with only 22 percent of those who did not take part.

### *(b) Full-Time Jobs*

The program was more helpful to girls than boys in getting better full-time jobs on leaving school. Among action group girls as a whole, 74 percent secured skilled or semi-skilled blue-collar or white-collar jobs, compared with 68 percent of control group girls. This is a small difference, but the spread is substantial between action group girls partially involved, 60 percent, and those actively involved, 91 percent. There is also a strong relation between intensity of participation and job level among boys, rising from 19 to 50 percent with level of involvement. The impact of intensity of participation on early full-time job level was strongest among low income youth and among those with low and high IQ scores.

The program helped non-British youth secure good full-time jobs even more than it did British youth. Among non-British in the experimental group 81 percent of those who were active succeeded in landing skilled blue or white collar jobs, compared with 31 percent of those partially involved and 53 percent of the non-British in the control group. We may conclude that while many children of immigrants completed school on their own, outside the intervention program, they tended more than others to rely on the project to get a better start in the work world.

Among young people in their early twenties, one-third of those who were partially involved secured skilled or white collar jobs but 71 percent who were active landed better jobs. This was due largely to the supervised work experience program. Some students who proved their worth at a job one school day a week walked into good full time jobs when they left school, often with the same employer.

### *(c) Perception of Problems in Transition to Work*

The programs helped girls more than boys in coping with the problems of transition from school to work. Of girls in the action group 84 percent said they had no troubles, compared with 59 percent of girls in the control group. The ease of transition rose with the intensity of participation. Boys had a little more trouble than girls, due no doubt to the fact that many girls were in business or commercial courses at school where conditions were quite similar to their new work situations. More boys entered jobs for which they were poorly prepared. However, the project eased transition for them too, particularly for those most actively engaged. Those from the poorest families were helped most to move from school to work; 87 percent of those in the action group said they had no problems as against 55 percent in the Eastside control group.

While youth at all three levels in IQ scores who were in the action group had less difficulty on the whole in moving into the work arena, compared with the control group, the greatest difference was among those with the highest scores. Of those with high scores in the action group 94 percent had no trouble in transition, compared with 50 percent of high scorers in the control group.

We might expect older youth to have fewer difficulties in settling into work, as other studies have found (Parnes 1971: 112; Committee on Youth, 1971). This was confirmed by our data, as six in ten of those 20 and older in the downtown control group said they had no problems, compared with four in ten of those under 19. But the difference by age disappeared among the action group, where three-quarters of all ages said they had a smooth passage.

### (d) Self-Confidence

The self-confidence of four in ten of the Experimental Group increased between middle and late adolescence, compared with three in ten of the Downtown Control Group. While the self-assurance of the action group was consistently greater than that of the control youth, there was not a systematic rise with increasing participation. Apparently being in the action, exposed even at a minimal level to its ideas and ethos, raised confidence.

Boys in both the action and control groups were much more confident than girls, and both sexes in the action group were substantially more confident than their counterparts in the control group.

Analysis by IQ score specifies the basic relation between participation and confidence. It is strongest among the brightest students, 82 percent in the action group and 50 percent in the control group. Their keener sense of the situation made them more responsive to the socializing experiences provided by the project.

### (e) Evaluation by Participants

Twice during the program youth in the Experimental Group evaluated it through anonymous questionnaires. In 88 completed responses immediately after the intervention phase, 70 percent stated that the programs had been somewhat or very helpful in completing school, while 60 percent said they had helped in some degree in maintaining interest and performance at school. At the same time 70 percent replied that the programs had been helpful in preparing for careers and 60 percent said that they had helped in finding and coping with their first jobs.

During late adolescence, evaluations were summarized in a single measure which included assistance in school completion, getting a good job, and becoming more mature. Among the 121 replies, 60 percent said the project had been somewhat or very helpful.

We completed 99 in-depth interviews in 1979–80, probing what experiences had been most and least helpful in attaining goals, and how they interpreted questions asked in earlier, structured interviews.

Mary is an example of those who recognize the long-term benefits of tutoring and part-time work at a large store. She had left school in October in the Twelfth Grade. Over the vice-principal's objections, the project arranged for her to return to school; workers advised her to get off welfare and move back with her parents. She recalled: "I wouldn't have finished Grade Twelve without the project's help in getting me a job and also a tutor who helped me in the spring so I could pass math." Later, as a result of the counselling program, she changed jobs. "I'm not disappointed I left my earlier job. I'm happy to be a government clerk."

Pat is an example of youth in the student employment program who dropped out. He left in Grade Ten and drives a truck. He is very dissatisfied and hopes to find a more fulfilling job. His opinion of the project, however, is highly positive:

> They let you go to work one day a week. I was with a utility company as a plumber's assistant. I loved it. One of the best jobs I ever had. In the summer I worked full-time. But I couldn't keep it because I left school.

Comments from others follow:

> "I got a part-time job from the centre at a large wholesaler. It led to my present full-time job in the shipping department. I've been there for six years ... "

> "They got me a part-time job when I was a student at a department store, then with a large distributing company. There I got my first experience doing typing and filing. I did enjoy the people there. I've been with another company as teller and receptionist for the past four years ... "

> "They got me a job with a paint works. It helped me get my head together."

Joan "had a good time" in the project. "It kept me out of trouble. I learned a lot about how to work in a large computerized office ... "

Lucy said: "The other workers as well as the boss encouraged me in the school-day I was released for a paying job. They got me started in the right direction ... It was good for the company, too. I did my best for them ... "

Glenna liked going out to various places. "This helped me decide what I really wanted to do. This chance should be open to all the kids."

Donna was one of the younger group who took part in the work experience program, in Grade Ten. "It worked out very well. I needed the money and learned a lot. It didn't interfere with my school work."

Laurie's people were among others who were enthusiastic about the employment program. She herself said: "It was very beneficial. I got the feeling of working with other people. And it made school more interesting."

John had a day's work a week with a large communication company. It made him want to go on to engineering college but he couldn't afford to. "After my parents talked with the project people, they persuaded me to go on and finish Grade Twelve; otherwise I would have quit in Ten."

Sonia said that she learned about social welfare programs and systems through the project. "I made connections, gained confidence, learned a lot, and people were nice."

## 5 / The Intervention Programs

Bill said "I was active in the project. It made you think about the future and yourself; planted seed in your mind."

Maria, an immigrant several years previously, had language difficulties and intended to drop out of a four-year course in spite of excellent marks. Eight months after working one school day a week for pay, she changed her mind and planned to finish the course. "I like the job, the people and the money. More kids should get the chance."

Ron said about his job: "I love it. I run different machines and do a good job. They're hiring me for the summer and want me back in the fall. I've changed my goal from being an auto mechanic to becoming a technician. I'll probably get a full-time job where I am now. My school marks are improving over last year. And do I love the four day week! School gets so boring by Grade Eleven."

Dave thought of other benefits. "I like the people. And I'm saving my money to go to Europe this summer." Dawn had wanted to finish high school but being in the program raised her goal to graduation from a community college. Before getting into the program, Jack had expected to leave school at the end of Grade Ten. After a drafting job with a public utility which he liked, he said that he wanted to become an engineer and would go to a polytechnical institute. His mother said that he had "come a little more alive" since joining the program.

Reports from employers were also favourable. Most noticed improvements not only in applied ability but in self-confidence and social skills.

Jane seemed shy and retiring at the beginning of her assignment but has become more friendly with the girls ... The work experience has put her into a different environment where she has to interact with more mature individuals. She is a conscientious person and applies herself very well ...

Whereas Heather seemed withdrawn at the outset, she adjusted rapidly to her new and strange surroundings ...

Jim's level of confidence seems to have significantly improved ...

During the summer Don will have a full-time job in accounting. This has been offered to him because of his good performance in my unit ...

We hope to send Michael to our plant school for additional training in the spring, preparing him for more complex work during the summer ...

Ken would most certainly have my support and recommendation if he were to apply for a permanent position in our company.

At the conclusion of the action phase of the project, students, parents, employers and educators recommended that work experience be continued in "Phase II." The Board of Education appointed a part-time coordinator for an experimental period, and the next year 85 students were admitted. Problems arose, however, because of lack of budget and inabil-

### Table 5-1: Young Adults Taking Courses, by Three Subsamples and by Sex* (Percentages)

|  | Downtown | | Uptown |
|---|---|---|---|
|  | *Experimental* | *Control* |  |
| Men | 31 | 18 | 36 |
| Women | 13 | 12 | 45 |
| Men and Women | 22 | 15 | 40 |
| Frequencies | (95) | (83) | (109) |

* Chi square = 3.31, 2 df, p = < .20.

ity of the coordinator to do the job on a half-time basis. There was also a difference in philosophy between the project leaders and Board administrators. Whereas the project specified that participants should be drop-out prone, Board officials insisted that work experience should be open only to students with good records and prospects — as a reward for performance. In addition, the provincial ministry of education still was not prepared to approve credits for part-time work experience for pay during school hours. Within two years the School Board terminated the project.

In a job market where there are too many unskilled youth and too many unfilled high skill job vacancies, student employment programs provide a situation where they can explore and choose a career and have an opportunity to test aptitudes and shape attitudes, a means of acquiring suitable work habits, and a chance to integrate and consolidate processes of learning in school and the larger community. We will return to this subject in the concluding chapter.

## Effects in Young Adulthood

By the time of the fourth interview, subjects were well into young adulthood, 23 to 25 years of age. One-half of the women and one-quarter of the Eastside men were married and three-quarters were working full-time; 7 percent were unemployed. Sixty-three percent of the Eastside women had full-time jobs; 6 percent were out of work. In Northend, 35 percent of the women had married, again twice the proportion of the men. Sixty-six percent of the uptown men were working full-time; 10 percent were unemployed. Among uptown women 53 percent had full-time jobs; only 2 percent were unemployed.

There was little overall change in the relative attainments in education and occupation of the sub-samples between late adolescence and young adulthood. But the benefits of active participation in the project were still evident. When youth took advantage of these opportunities the effects of relative deprivation in most cases were substantially diminished.

One change is of particular significance in young adulthood. From Table 5–1 we see that men who had been active in the project were more likely than their counterparts in the downtown control group to take post-secondary courses. Their re-entry into education and training demonstrates the long-range benefits of the project. The fact that men more than women returned to post-secondary education is no doubt due partly to the different requirements for advancement in employment. Downtown women tended to be in low to middle level, white or blue-collar jobs; advancement was chiefly by on-job experience and training. Promotion for men required community college courses to a larger degree. In contrast, Northend women surged ahead of men in taking post-secondary courses at university or college.

These findings show the necessity of continuing longitudinal research into young adulthood if we are to understand clearly the transition of youth into work. Intervention, even at the rather late stage of middle adolescence, has lasting benefits.

# 6

# Entry Job and Satisfaction

We may now summarize the critical early stages of young adults' work status and the satisfactions it yields in the two areas under study. Findings have implications for further research and for developing policy to prepare the young for productive and satisfying adulthood.

## Path Models of Attainment

To this point we have used two and three-way analysis to unravel the selection and preparation process. In this chapter we use a single measure that takes account of the cumulative effects of a series of variables on status outcomes. Multiple regression by path analysis is efficient for this purpose, testing the model set out in Figure 1–1 in Chapter 1. The model posits these stages: background factors, socialization in early, middle and late adolescence, intermediate outcomes and final outcomes in young adulthood. These are educational and occupational attainment and satisfaction at entry into full-time work. Results may differ from those yielded by earlier, simpler analysis, chiefly because of the cumulative feature of the models.

Table 6–1 shows the standardized Beta coefficients for major, significantly related, *antecedents of educational level* downtown in Eastside. This is a powerful model, explaining 57 percent of the variance in educational attainment among Eastside young adults, now 23 to 25 years of age. It compares in predictive strength with such studies as the large scale, pioneering one of Wisconsin youth by Sewell and associates (1970). Using a slightly different model, they explained 54 percent of the variance in educational attainment. Our model demonstrates the strong effect of the Ontario selection system through tracking. But it also shows the greater importance of high school performance and educational expectation. They surpass measured intelligence in predicting "success" at the post-secondary level.

## Table 6-1: Downtown Young Adults, Significant Variables Regressed on Educational Attainment

| Antecedents | Standardized Beta Coefficients |
|---|---|
| School Performance, Grades 9, 10 | .320 |
| Educational Expectation, Grades 9, 10 | .298 |
| Track (Academic) | .281 |
| Intelligence Quotient, Grades 9, 10 | .189 |

What gives rise to *school performance* in Grades Nine and Ten, which is so important for outcomes down the way? The downtown model for performance is weak, explaining only 9 percent of the variance (not shown). However, it shows as significant antecedents non-British ethnicity (.225) and occupation of father (.203). The latter recurs in most studies of youth's transition to work, parents' status acting indirectly through intervening variables, as is the case here. In Eastside an even stronger determinant of school performance is minority ethnicity. Immigrant families bring enormous pressure to bear on their children to achieve, largely through the avenue of continued education. Intelligence scores were not sufficiently strong to be included in this model. While the model is weak, indicating that other unspecified variables were at work to produce school performance, the convergence of parental occupation and ethnic origin points to cultural factors as critical ones for school performance, compared with individual characteristics.

*Educational expectation* is the second strongest predictor of educational level, as shown in Table 6–1; it reflects individual choice to a large extent. Three earlier variables combine to explain 42 percent of variance in expectation (not shown): academic track (.424), Grade Nine and Ten performance (.246) and intelligence score (.195). Expectation sums up the subjective response of individuals to the objective indicators of their probable future place in society. Findings show that for most youth it is not enough to be born into privilege. The individual must believe in his or her future place and strive towards it, chiefly through commitment to schooling, with the inner discipline that this entails.

There are, of course, many exceptions to the dictum of commitment to educational achievement. One can point to unusual persons who are "successful" in traditional or innovative careers without staying at school. And many who go through all the "right" motions — as prescribed by dominant elder groups — do not attain eminent life stations. However, we

### Table 6-2: Downtown Young Adults, Significant Variables Regressed on Job Level

| Antecedents | Standardized Beta Coefficients |
| --- | --- |
| Educational Attainment | .457 |
| Sex (Female) | .322 |
| Self-Confidence, Late Adolescence, Ages 19-20 | .183 |

describe here normal patterns of advancement in the downtown area that, for the majority, lead to social positions.

To complete the early status cycle, we turn now to the model of *job level* among young adults in Eastside. This is summed up in Table 6–2. This is a moderately strong model, explaining 36 percent of the variance in occupational level reached by downtown young adults, in their early twenties. By far the leading predictor is educational level, confirming findings of many other enquiries. Factors we have shown as leading to educational level may be taken as contributing also, indirectly, to the level of job achieved.

But two new factors appear in this equation: sex, a strong predictor, and self-confidence in late adolescence, a weaker but also consistent predictor. Girls in Eastside have acquired higher status jobs than their male cohorts, measuring status by conventional criteria such as prestige and security. Remember, however, that most Eastside girls are in "female-prescribed" roles, with little prospect of rising into higher, decision-making roles. Not many are self-employed or are well paid. They have cleaner tasks, usually, than downtown men, but do not often break into senior, "male-prescribed" circles. Self-confidence is more common among young men, and this sustains some of them in their drive toward better-paying, more gratifying positions.

When we turn to *Northend* young adults, the models are more complex. In Table 6–3 we see that three antecedents are significantly related to *educational attainment*. These variables together explain 36 percent of the variance in educational level, providing a moderately strong model. The foremost influence in Northend is track; students in the academic track, usually now at the advanced level, are most likely to go on to post-secondary education. Next in importance is school performance in Grades Nine and Ten, and third is job expectation.

### Table 6-3: Uptown Young Adults, Significant Variables Regressed on Educational Level

| Antecedents | Standardized Beta Coefficients |
|---|---|
| Track (Academic) | .353 |
| School Performance, Grades 9, 10 | .295 |
| Job Expectation in Mid-Adolescence | .146 |

Measured intelligence enters indirectly into the Northend equation, as it does downtown. But instead of educational expectation, which was in second place downtown, job expectation is significant uptown.

Interestingly, school track uptown is significantly related also to *job expectation*, thus, indirectly raising its total effect on educational attainment. High IQ score does not appear in the equation; it has an indirect effect on attainment through job expectation. Similarly, parental background acts indirectly on educational attainment uptown, though with an unanticipated twist. Young people whose parents had *less* than average income and education but who were upwardly mobile, perform better and have higher job expectation than others.

An important difference between areas arises in the formation of school performance, or marks, in Grades Nine and Ten. Downtown we saw that IQ score does not make it directly to this equation, which has weak predictive power. Uptown, however, the equation accounts for 38 percent of variance in performance — a moderate model (not shown). IQ score uptown is a strong correlate of marks, with a coefficient of .514, followed by sex, with a coefficient of .320. Girls are higher school achievers in Northend than boys — which does not happen downtown. Ethnicity makes no difference uptown, though it does downtown. Further, Northend youth from lower income homes did better in Grades Nine and Ten than those from higher income families. All of this confirms the evidence from simpler two-way correlations in earlier chapters that different forces are at work in the two areas. Uptown, the academic track gives middle-class youth more opportunity for individual advancement than the academic track does downtown. In spite of school efforts there, the burden of poverty, institutionalized in the family, is usually too heavy for individual ability and effort to dislodge.

Table 6–4 represents a complex pattern of *job attainment among Northend young adults*; six variables have significant cumulative effects on jobs attained by young adults, aged 23 to 25. It is a fairly strong model,

### Table 6-4: Uptown Young Adults, Significant Variables Regressed on Job Level

| Antecedents | Standardized Beta Coefficients |
|---|---|
| School Track (Academic) | -.465 |
| Educational Attainment | .443 |
| Educational Expectation, Grades 9, 10 | .363 |
| Sex (girls) | .309 |
| Part-Time Jobs During High School | -.250 |
| Job Expectation, Mid-Adolescence | -.193 |

accounting for 42 percent of the variance. Three of the relationships are negative, that is, low scores in the antecedents lead to high scores in job levels. The negative coefficient with track means that those who had been in the academic track have at present low level jobs because many have only temporary work while continuing their education. The negative coefficient with part-time jobs means that those who worked part-time while in school have low level jobs — not surprising in Northend where, at the time, no school-related or coop education courses were available. The negative coefficient for job expectations means, again, that those who are aiming at high level jobs are not yet through college or university; their jobs at the time are temporary and at a low level.

Two of the positive coefficients in the uptown equation for job level are similar to the two strongest antecedents for downtown job level: educational attainment and sex. But whereas downtown the third positive coefficient is between occupation and self-confidence, in the uptown sample it is with educational expectation. This suggests that in the lower income area, with limited access to higher positions, those who do well in early job advancement — though at a relatively lower level — bring to bear a self-assurance that partly offsets restricted job goals. Uptown youth, however, have higher job expectations, which raise systematically their realistic chances for higher levels of job attainment.

## Job Satisfaction

A number of studies have shown that certain forms of work satisfaction are associated with productivity, initiative and self-fulfilment (Deci, 1972; King, Murray and Atkinson, 1979; Vroom, 1964). We enquired into general, extrinsic and intrinsic job satisfaction and their possible sources in the three sub-samples. *General satisfaction* is a diffuse concept of well-being related to having a job with reasonable rewards. It is widely distributed among late adolescents in the three samples, especially for men, 49 to 55 percent being satisfied and 30 to 33 percent being "very satisfied," with the higher ratios among uptown workers. But whereas 31 percent of women in the downtown control group were very satisfied, 40 percent of those in the experimental group and 50 percent of uptown women were.

Pay and job status were not systematically associated with general satisfaction in either area. Rather, for Eastside late adolescents, this outcome was associated significantly only with what they hope to be working at some day and their self-confidence. For Northend late adolescents, it is related with expected education and position. Hence, it is an idealized concept, part of a youthful, optimistic syndrome.

*Intrinsic satisfaction*, however, is a more specific reality, based on a positive response to the work process itself; it registers opportunity for creativity, responsibility and freedom. Interviewees aged 17 and 18 were asked to state what type of satisfaction they anticipated in preferred positions, intrinsic or extrinsic, the latter including pay, conditions and companions. Downtown, 59 percent of men opted for intrinsic benefits, compared with 74 percent of uptown men. But 67 percent of the downtown experimental group women chose intrinsic benefits, compared with 60 percent of downtown control women and 90 percent of uptown women. *Apparently women in the action group anticipated inward satisfactions more than cohorts in their area, though not so much as uptown cohorts.*

In the combined downtown sample, intrinsic satisfaction anticipated in preferred jobs is significantly related with both educational and occupational attainment. It is expected that higher achievement will be rewarded with inward satisfaction. A clustering of other related variables indicates a normative viewpoint; job expectation, academic track and family church-going characterize youth who persistently seek and expect intrinsic satisfaction (Appendix B). In contrast, the roots of intrinsic satisfaction among uptown youth are diffuse. There the only antecedent variable moderately related with intrinsic satisfaction is sex; Northend young women are more intrinsically oriented than men (Appendix C).

## Implications for Theory and Policy

We may now highlight several findings that have important implications for theories of transition and for policies that may enhance chances for youth to make a good beginning in productive and satisfying careers.

(a) For the large majority of youth in both the working and middle class areas, the data show that the necessary last step to promising and fulfilling jobs is the *completion at least of secondary school and preferably post-secondary education.* Schools continue to play a crucial role in the selection and preparation of youth for positions in the stratification system. For some young people schools open up a better way of life and for others they effectively close the door of opportunity. This observation is reached in virtually all recent North American studies of education's role in transition.

(b) The next most important factor in the attainment of positions is the *initiative of the individual* through intellectual ability and effort. Intelligence is the product of genetic and cultural endowment and of early socialization in the family, school, and community. In actual fact, as noted in the Introduction, it is not a background variable in the same way that socio-economic status is, because, while the latter is part of the environment at the time of birth, intellectual ability is strongly conditioned by interaction with others after birth. But for the purposes of this study, the designation of IQ score as a background factor is valid since we began observations when youth were at the age of 13 to 15 years. They had already been sorted for different learning environments and social destinations, partly on the basis of IQ scores in elementary school!

We have shown that individual effort is the cumulative response to learning situations and influential others. It is expressed in school performance and expectation for education and jobs. *The intervention program demonstrated that it is possible to raise the performance and plans of certain youth for education and occupation by modifying the learning environment, with the cooperation of school personnel, families, and employers.*

(c) By the time a person reaches adolescence, *the socio-economic status of parents* affects school and work attainment chiefly through intervening variables, the most important being educational ones. The total impact of SES, including endowment and early socialization, though difficult to measure, is critical. For example, it operates partly through neighbourhoods which are largely homogeneous by class and which strongly affect formal and informal learning. The process of class segmentation reaches a fateful juncture by Grade Eight, when children at present are tracked into schools or programs which have specialized goals, although it functions also at early grades through enrichment or remedial programs. Parental SES also operates on education through differing rates of secondary completion and support for post-secondary schooling. Background status affects job hopes, plans, and actions structurally by contacts, openings and support, and psychologically through access to models, value formation, and counselling.

(d) The powerful place of *school track* in the overall transitional process has been demonstrated. It constitutes intervention by public education into the learning and eventually the careers of the young. The philosophy and purposes behind this intervention have not been widely discussed in Canada but social scientists have concluded that it tends to maintain elitist privileges (Porter, Porter and Blishen, 1973/82; Pike, 1970; Breton, 1972; Gilbert, 1979; Anisef, 1975, 1982; Boyd and associates, 1985; Crysdale, King and Mandell, forthcoming).

(e) The established attainment order is *being challenged, however, by two ascending groups: non-British minorities and young women.* The two sample areas differ widely in this respect, for minority ethnicity appeared as an influential background variable downtown while uptown it is girls who are setting the pace in education and job level. The ambiguous prospects for minority youth are indicated by contradictions in outcomes. Downtown, in spite of handicaps in parental education, income and in expressed intelligence scores, minority youth surpass the British majority in school performance, tracking into an academic program, and attainment in education. But, at the time of the last inclusive survey, during late adolescence, they were only equal to British origin youth in job attainment. Uptown, they also were at a disadvantage in background and were unable to reverse this position later in performance, school or job attainment, wages, job mobility or job satisfaction.

(f) The *gender* revolution has not yet affected school and job attainment downtown, apart from youth in the experimental group. Control group girls leave school sooner than boys in spite of their almost equal performance. Girls in the downtown control sample lag behind in returning for post-secondary courses. They attain higher job status than boys by a gross prestige scale but, in fact, their white collar jobs often are at a low level. They sag badly in self-confidence and are far behind in wages. In spite of this, they do not differ from men in general job satisfaction. In contrast, uptown girls surpass boys in school performance, in hopes, plans, and in educational and job attainment. They fall drastically behind men in wages and in self-confidence. But they are slightly better pleased than men with their jobs and tend much more to stress intrinsic aspects of work. Although we did not explore this aspect of gender in this study, other studies show that male-favouring barriers still exist in most schools and they are even higher in many places of employment (Mandell and Crysdale, 1993).

(g) The impact of *ethnicity is complex but consistently significant*. It varies by social class and neighbourhood. Downtown minority youth, especially Oriental and Asians, are strongly motivated to attain, but uptown they are slightly surpassed by dominant Anglo cohorts.

(h) *The most cogent difference between the area models has to do with the degree to which individual and structural variables interact to bring about the two critical outcomes, educational and occupational attainment.* Individual characteristics, such as IQ score, sex, and educational and job expectations, have much greater impact on outcomes uptown than downtown. It appears that uptown mobility is based on individual "contest," while downtown mobility to a greater degree is structurally and psychologically "conditioned." In some respects, at late adolescence, we observed among downtown youth a greater measure of independence from others, including school personnel and parents, in comparison with uptown youth. But this was of no avail in the sorting process, based partly on tracking in early adolescence and school retention in middle adolescence.

The disadvantages of being raised downtown, stemming from background, environment and experience, are only partly offset by the return of some for post-secondary education. The intervention program had an extended influence in encouraging a higher proportion of young people who were active to return for more courses. But once more uptown youth in much larger proportions benefit from continuing education. In general, "conditioned mobility," in which schools track most Eastside youth into shorter, applied programs at the secondary level, often regardless of mental ability and ambition, works to their disadvantage.

# 7
# Values, Beliefs and Attainment

It is clear that values and beliefs have a strong effect on behaviour for most people most of the time. Like most studies of education and transition, the foregoing discussion takes for granted the formation of goals and their implementation in the passage to adulthood and employment. But because of the increasingly crucial nature of transition for individuals and society it has become urgent to understand more fully the relation between norms and behaviour. Most studies concentrate on the effects of structural factors such as social class, gender, ethnicity, influential others and school experience to explain occupational destination and status. They omit consideration of values because of difficulties in conceptualization and operationalization. But the result is to distort reality.

At mid-stage in analysis we attempted to quantify values but were only partly successful due to the complexity of the concept and the primitive state of the art. Nevertheless, we report here some interesting findings based on observation, both quantitative and qualitative. In the former we must rely on two-way, or zero-order correlation and, in the latter, case studies. Descriptive data are unusually rich, gathered in 99 in-depth interviews with young adults after more than ten years of structured enquiry. Because of limited numbers we cannot generalize widely but for the samples the results are reliable and valid.

Theories of social psychologists are helpful. Erik Erikson (1963) observed that youth in modern societies commonly experience identity confusion, which is largely resolved when they become fully employed and take on responsible adult roles. Internalized values or orientations that are in accord with approved behaviourial patterns lead to strengthened and satisfying identities. The work of Jean Piaget (1969), Lawrence Kohlberg (1964) and others on the development of cognition and moral judgement assumes that the adoption of hierarchies of goals or values leads to attainments. These goals are commonly reached by stages.

### Table 7-1: Normative Orientations, Two Areas, Late Adolescents (Percentages)

|  | Downtown | Uptown |
|---|---|---|
| The Most Important Problem People Face Today: | | |
|   Individual, interpersonal, transcendental concerns | 27 | 36 |
|   Social concerns | 73 | 64 |
|   *Frequencies* | (174) | (107) |
| How the Most Important Problem Should Be Addressed: | | |
|   Pragmatic orientation | 46 | 38 |
|   Ideological orientation | 54 | 62 |
|   *Frequencies* | (151) | (100) |
| Degree That Beliefs Affect Actions: | | |
|   Little or not at all | 24 | 17 |
|   Moderately | 23 | 23 |
|   Greatly | 52 | 60 |
|   *Frequencies* | (162) | (101) |

## Normative Variables in Two Areas

Following Milton Yinger's (1970) now classic method, we asked young adults two questions about values: "What, in your opinion, is the most important issue people face today?" and "How should this problem be solved?" Answers to the first question about the major problem fall into two broad groups: *individualistic or social*. This distinction does not have the explanatory power of the answers to the second question. Table 7-1 compares normative tendencies in the downtown and uptown areas.

Answers for the second question fall into two main types: *ideological* and *pragmatic*. Ideologues have a compelling commitment to an underlying set of principles on which they base behaviour. There is a tendency toward consistency in moral action in both personal and social situations. In the following sections we show that ideologues try to implement their beliefs about desirable ends in educational and occupational attainment. Pragmatists, in contrast, do not rely on consistent normative orientations but suit actions to changing situations, placing self-interest ahead of social obligations. They tend not to be strongly committed to socially prescribed goals in education or occupation. We do not judge which is right or wrong. In restrictive circumstances of upbringing and experience, how can

## 7 / Values, Beliefs and Attainment

the observer be sure of what is absolutely right for others? It could be for some a matter of survival, as they see it — the best or only way they perceive as leading out of a formidable moral dilemma.

The table also compares for the two areas a third normative tendency: *Belief efficacy*. This shows the degree to which youth think that they can practise their beliefs in studies and work. Because we did not include this variable in the early interviews we cannot use it in analysis of the entire samples. We did include it in the 99 in-depth interviews and are able to apply it in this chapter, on the effects of values and beliefs on attainments. (The effects of values on transitional outcomes are also discussed in a larger survey in 1990-91 by Crysdale, King and Mandell, forthcoming).

The most striking feature of this table is the similarity of normative tendencies in the two areas; the differences are also interesting. A large proportion of youth in both areas select social concerns as most important, though more in the middle class area are individualistic. Social concerns include economic and political questions, justice, peace and the environment. The more privileged youth uptown to a larger degree are apt to stress such personal questions as love, cooperation, understanding, self-awareness and openness. Preferred solutions (based on the second question) indicate the belief — ethical orientation of youth. A majority in both areas express faith in ideological solutions, as against pragmatism.

We looked at the relations between individualism and central outcomes in the design and found few statistically significant relations. These did exist for downtown youth who had been in academic programs in high school, whose occupational aims were high, who were active in secondary associations and were pragmatists. Uptown individualists usually had reached high educational levels but as other outcomes most relevant for this study were not affected, we discontinued this line of enquiry.

*Ideology*, however, was systematically related with several relevant outcomes in both areas. Downtown these included being of non-British origin and having fathers who attended church regularly (Appendix B). Uptown ideologues are likely to have fathers with low occupational status; they came to this country with little more than optimistic ideals and many of their youth have retained high hopes. They also said that they were closely attached to both parents. They were apt to belong to churches and to attend services regularly. On the whole they were satisfied with their jobs, though they were not upwardly mobile up to that time (Appendix C).

A finer examination by type of ideology reveals correlations with achievement which are not apparent in the foregoing analysis.

### Table 7-2: Types of Ideology in Two Areas, Youth Aged 21-23 (Percentages)

|  | Downtown | Uptown | Totals |
|---|---|---|---|
| Humanistic | 26 | 36 | 28 |
| Political | 18 | 10 | 15 |
| Religious | 9 | 15 | 11 |
| Pragmatic (non-ideological) | 46 | 38 | 45 |
| *Totals, %* | 99 | 99 | 99 |
| *N* | (65) | (34) | (99) |

## Types of Ideologues

Various forms of ideology affect outcomes differently. The distribution of the in-depth sample in the two areas by type of ideology is shown in Table 7–2.

*Downtown* the largest proportion of "ideologues" have humanistic ideals; they believe that the most acute human problems can be resolved or at least eased by moral behaviour on a wide scale but in quite general terms. The second largest group of downtown ideologues believe in political efficacy; the worst problems require political policies and programs. A smaller number call for the application of religious beliefs: "change the person and heal the world." But almost one-half are pragmatists; basic problems are either insolvable or beyond understanding. Certainly they would not feel committed to solutions.

*Uptown* the largest group of ideologues also are humanists, but the second largest group are not politically but religiously committed. In this middle class area over one-third, compared with almost one-half of the working class downtown, are not ideological at all but pragmatic. They test the wind; in each situation they serve first their own interest, though most would not act in direct violation of fundamental human rights.

In this discussion we think of "ideal types" in the tradition of Max Weber (Hekman, 1983). Although based on empirical grounds, probabilities of taking ideological or pragmatic positions that affect personal and social action cannot be expected to occur in every case or situation. But tendencies in these directions are sufficiently common to justify the construction of typologies.

Another difference between areas is in the degree to which interviewees said that beliefs affect everyday actions (Table 7-1). For a slightly higher percentage of uptown youth, beliefs "greatly" affect their behaviour and fewer think that the impact is "little or not at all." In their more affluent situation, they have more room to manoeuvre in moral behaviour. They have a greater sense of power in dealing with ambiguities or contradictions at school and at work.

Relatively small numbers, as we have stated, restrict the generalizability of these findings, but they are grounded on observed facts. Further evidence of these tendencies is presented in the next section on case studies of moral positions in relation to background and transitional behaviour.

## Orientations and Correlates: Eastside Sketches

### (a) Downtown Humanists

Seymour thinks that the most urgent problem facing people is getting along in the family; the best way to deal with this is for husbands and wives to compromise and love one another. He should know, as his parents were alcoholics and fought all the time. When the family fell apart, he moved out and still lives alone. One reason is that he is a baker and works many nights, which cuts down on his social life.

He was often in despair as a child. He went to a vocational school and there a teacher suggested he consider becoming a baker. This was a turning point. The Eastside Youth Project took a group through a hotel and he was fascinated by what was happening in the kitchen. He now is a pastry chef in a prestigious restaurant and hopes someday to open his own shop. He is very satisfied with his work and is upwardly mobile. His satisfaction is intrinsic. Further, he projects his values. "I'd like to do something to make the world better for kids."

At one time he joined a religious sect but doesn't attend now because of his work. Religion for him is believing in God and living a moral life. He practises what he believes most of the time. "Education means a lot to those who want to get somewhere. It should combine theories with practice."

Jennie is a listener, she says. Like Seymour she thinks that the most important problem is learning to live together. She adds, "I really don't know how to help people do this, but I try to practise my beliefs in the way I treat people." Her family was a close one and they went to church every Sunday. She prays every night but doesn't go to church now. She is happily married.

She works as a sales secretary for a medium size firm and is very satisfied with her work. While she likes her companions the chief advantage is to earn money. She's not interested in advancement. Education means for her the best way to get a good job.

Maria came to this country from southern Europe when she was small. Her parents went only to Grade Six and were not able to help her much because of the language. She dropped out in Grade Nine. She worked for a while in accounts receivable for a service business and recently was made assistant office manager. She is very satisfied and likes the work mostly because it is interesting, although she adds that the money is good. For her the major world problem is getting jobs and earning money. The solution? "Have faith in people ... give them a chance."

She never really liked school; all her friends left without completing a diploma. "They weren't interested in us and we weren't interested in them." The main purpose of education is to get a good job. The ideal school would combine work experience with other subjects. "My beliefs affect my work a little ... I work hard and am truly honest." She usually goes to church. "I'm glad to be a Catholic."

Santos went through Grade Twelve and is now back trying Thirteen part-time. There was a lot of tension at home when he was growing up. His immigrant parents had little education and tried to get him to leave earlier and go to work. "Get a job and get married," his father said. "He was no help. He drank all the time and was off work a lot. Mother didn't understand life here and she worked nights." The big issue for Santos is the lack of good friends. The solution is for us all to be more open. He does his best to put his beliefs into practice. His parents were very religious but they didn't live it. He is indifferent. "I'm an agnostic or fatalist. Who needs religion?"

While going to school, he works part-time as a taxi despatcher. Education means to become enlightened, to better yourself, and to prepare for a good job. "I'd like to have an interesting job, but I'm not sure what it will be ... The ideal school would be quite traditional, emphasizing basic knowledge, but also introducing you to work, and the discipline should be strict."

### *(b) Downtown Political Ideologues*

Lucille is married; she and her husband own a house in Eastside, where she was raised. She is concerned about bringing up her child there as it's dirty, noisy and tough. She left school in Grade 10, as for years she had been in a foster home and didn't have any interest in school. "I hated to read; still do. Mother and dad quarrelled and finally separated. He was

French and she was Irish. Just before he died he told mom where we were and she came and got us together again. She did her best but it was hard; she worked as a cleaner in a government building."

As Lucy had taken typing at school, she got a job and worked up to be office manager. "Work changed my life. I found I could do things pretty well and developed self-confidence." Now she works part-time. Her satisfaction is intrinsic — the job itself is challenging, but, of course, the money is also important.

The major issue is the economy and the only way to improve conditions is for the government to have programs to stimulate production. At election time she works for her party. "I have a real concern for justice," she says, "and I practise the work ethic. Guess it's because I had such a tough start." Again, "Politics in this area are in bad shape. A lot could be done to help people, but money is wasted on useless things ... But I won't get involved myself ... Well, maybe I would if I was called upon."

Values are important to Lucy, and they evidently affect her life in different areas. She doesn't go to church because as a youngster she found it so boring. But "once in a while" she prays. "I believe in God. I guess I have morals. I wouldn't cheat, except at cards."

Education should lead to knowledge and self-satisfaction. She was very insecure at school. Kids laughed at her because of a disfigurement. She never got to like school. The most important aspect of education is preparing you for a job. "I needed encouragement and counselling and didn't get either ... In an ideal school teachers would care for you and you'd like them. My parents were too busy to care. Lucky for me my older brothers looked out for me ... saw that I was home and OK for the night."

Another example of overcoming early obstacles and having a political orientation is provided by Jude. He finished Grade 12 but it was in a vocational school, which didn't prepare him for anything. "I was slow and they put me in a low level school; I know that I could have handled a higher level but nobody listened. It was so boring." His father treated him like dirt and never helped him at school or getting work. He urged him to quit school and go to work at anything he could get.

During the interview his father yelled at him, and though 23, he jumped. When the father left Jude apologized to the interviewer. "I get along well with mother, but then, she works and, anyway, what dad says goes." He drifted from job to job and, with ex-school mates, began drinking heavily whenever they could. It was their only pleasure. A couple of them got into drugs and committed suicide. There was nothing for them.

Then a friend spoke for him at a shipping firm and he got his first decent job, as a night shipper. Now he is making good money and is proud. His girl friend is a Christian and he goes to church with her. He stopped drinking and helps her at a drop-in centre for youth where she works. His face lights up when he talks of their coming marriage. He'd like to work at something that would make life better for people.

The main problem facing people, Jude thinks, is unemployment and lack of money. "Maybe a socialist government would do better. I'm not sure ... What does education mean to me? Nothing. You go through school and you're not prepared for anything. Can't get a job, so you go on welfare. Sports kept me in school. I was good at them. But the certificate I got won't get me into post-secondary. It's useless. In the ideal system there would be no vocational schools. They should all be academic and children encouraged to study. There should be equal opportunity ... I'm a better person because of the sad experiences I went through. I have faith, try to be honest and have respect for others."

Kirk also had an unpromising start. He left Grade 12 with bitterness because he didn't like English. He loved science but couldn't stand other parts of school. His parents were not helpful. They had little education and his father made it painfully clear he did not like his son. He worked at odd jobs for several years before going as a mature student to community college. An uncle and aunt encouraged him, and he got a student loan. Now he's studying polymer science and is in the third year. He hopes to go to university and study radio chemistry. He works in the library until midnight, then goes home to sleep.

The major issue for Kirk is employment, and political action is needed to provide solutions. His beliefs, which are moral and not religious, do guide him and help keep him studying toward his goals. It is hard for him to practise what he preaches. He quips: "I follow the golden rule ... do to others what they do to you." Kirk thinks that education should lead to an occupation but it also makes the individual more knowledgeable and reasoning. The perfect school would teach the three Rs and introductory work skills. Teachers would take a personal interest in students. He definitely considers that the most satisfying thing at work is not money or friends but enjoyment with what you are doing.

### (c) *Downtown Religious Ideologues*

Lin came to Canada with her parents from Hong Kong when she was small. They never went past Grade Eight but she stayed on and finished university. She lives at home but is not close to her parents; she's always been afraid of her father. She thinks that the major issue is social relations at personal and international levels. "The best solution is for people to become Christian." She belongs to a Chinese Gospel Church which is trying to make this happen. She's in a leadership training group there and enjoys its solidarity. Her beliefs strongly affect her actions.

She's not satisfied with her present job as a cost control accountant and is taking further courses toward a higher level. What she'd really like to do is teach but there aren't many openings. The people she works with now are unpleasant.

"I always liked school; it was my own ambition drove me on. Education is broadening and fits you for a better job. It should stimulate learning in different ways. Among other things it should help you get along with others. My faith does this. My family and friends were not interested in religion although now mom and dad go to church with me."

Tom is also an active Christian, though he started off in another direction. "The biggest world problem is that people lie and cheat; they've turned away from God. The answer is to change your life and go straight ... I know. I tried it the other way and it didn't work. I tried to escape my father who was a religious fanatic and violent. He travelled and preached all over the continent. When he was home we had to study the Bible two hours a day. If we didn't pay attention he'd hit you with a belt and if you cried he'd hit you again. If you were bad you had to kneel on bent rods and hold up a chair. I did this until I was old enough to beat him up.

> When I was 16 we had an honest talk. He argued that it was my mother's fault that things went wrong. I tried to understand and changed my attitude; I love my parents. On her side she always had to work at low jobs, as she hadn't much schooling. She really supported us and still works as a cleaner. She did her best although there didn't seem to be any real affection. I live with her now.

> You can understand father. He was in a concentration camp during the war. Terrible things happened. Later he had to go into a mental hospital. Mother was in a work camp, too. Dad tried to strangle me once and I fought him off.

> My brothers are doing well in business and I'd like to get into it, too. But I failed Grade 10 because I didn't like history ... An ideal school? It should increase knowledge, sharpen thinking, improve communication, help you get a good job. Now all I can do is drive a truck. It's lousy, but in my middle 20's it's too late to get more education.

I try to practise my beliefs. I lead a group of kids. My faith is my life. Before I was turning into garbage.

Paul is another youth of minority ethnic background with a difficult start. After a troubled adolescence, he also is now a religious ideologue. He's strongly motivated to become a priest who serves people; he's on his way, having almost completed a degree in philosophy. He was a gifted student at high school who rarely studied but took home high grades. He was bored and made trouble. He drank and was on drugs ... almost died of a deliberate overdose. His father, whom he adored, suffered from a terminal disease and his mother worked hard all day and drank hard at night.

He couldn't express what he thought is the top problem for people and couldn't find a simple answer. But the direction to take is by love, faith and caring. What he thinks of again and again is the patience his father had during his illness. Paul waited on him as best he could. When he died there was a gnawing emptiness. "But you have to go on ... sometimes you win, sometimes you lose...

"We were immigrants, like most of our neighbours. We were people without a country. Teenagers in a lower class area, we were all trying to get out, to pursue middle class values. We formed gangs, took drugs, didn't know what the hell we were doing. Even today, when I work at odd jobs to support my studies, there's a constant threat of eviction...

"My father left his first family for my mother. Perhaps this shouldn't have happened and I shouldn't have been born. We've all turned out badly ... My sister kicked me out of my own house...

"It took a long time after father died to get myself together — three years. I fought my family, friends, school, everything. Then on a canoe trip I felt the presence of God, there in the peace and beauty all around ... I went to mass with my grandfather and he talked of his simple faith. I'm still a sinner, but I hope to be a good Catholic, who knows and follows Christ. It will take a long time ... My beliefs make all the difference.

"What's the purpose of education? Not what I thought, to help me become better than the people I used to think were friends. Education shouldn't be competitive; we should help each other grow as persons. Education is life experience ... We should be earnestly committed to learning for learning's sake, to seek the truth. Our teachers were fair; we were dolts. But it wasn't until I tried to end life that I started to like it. I came to realize I didn't hate my family. I didn't take to religion because I was downtrodden. I took to it because I had a revelation. Now I know where I'm heading."

## *(d) Downtown Pragmatists*

Sue, who has worked as a printer in a factory for five years, is essentially a pragmatist. The big problem is dollars, or the lack of them. She doesn't know what can be done about it. She was expelled from school in Grade Ten, the same level as her parents had reached. She's quite satisfied with her job, although she would like to be supervisor as her pay is quite low. Her people both worked at low level jobs and spent the weekends at a neighbouring pub. They didn't care that she had been expelled; it was no disgrace. In fact, they didn't talk much with the kids about anything.

Her husband, a city works operator, listened to the interview and interrupted several times to correct her. When he and his buddies start talking about current affairs it turns her off. What does education mean to her? "Not much. I was never read to and I don't like reading now...

"Do my values affect my actions? Well, I'm honest. My chief interest, beside the kids, is my job. We need the money. But the work is interesting and the company doesn't treat me like a slave ... I am not much interested in religion or politics. Once I got to be a teenager, I found better things to do than go to church. My husband was brought up Catholic but doesn't go. Even the minister who married us didn't seem too friendly. He didn't invite us to go to his church. I believe in God. That's it!"

Siumay is a freelance graphic artist; she works part-time as a receptionist. It brings in cash. Life is simple; she lives alone in a flat downtown. She loves her work but would prefer to be in fine art. The major issue for her is the obsession of so many with middle-class, materialistic values. The solution would be to involve more people in critical action.

Unlike Sue, whose parents were indifferent toward her, Siu's problem was that her parents tried to dominate her. She couldn't discuss things she was interested in with them as they had little education and were overly dependent on traditional Chinese values. Her mother was a strong individual but tried to perpetuate the myth of subservient womanhood. She was Buddhist and he was an atheist; this caused a lot of strife. Her father tried to maintain ethnic distinctness, which she found unacceptable. "It was hell. Finally I moved out ... Family is something to shake off, like a snake's skin."

While she graduated from community college in art, she found education restrictive. "It's too formal and abstract. Instead of sticking all to books, teachers should help students learn more from life. The best way to cope with education is to negate it, question it, challenge it. We should set our own principles and beliefs ... Beliefs are constantly changing. But we need them to stand up against pressures to mechanize, isolate and empty humanity of real meaning. While I haven't a church, I believe in God. My mother's Buddhist rites are simple, sincere and peaceful...

"At college I finally came to realize that, in a way, I had been lied to all my life by my parents and teachers. I couldn't depend on anyone else or any set of ideas to really guide me. On my own, mistakes I make are my own mistakes and I really learn from them. I prefer living freely, without a full-time job, though I'm near the poverty line. This way I can talk with others but finally it's up to me."

Most pragmatists are not so self-complete. Roland went to Grade Eleven, about the same level as his parents. He was very close to his father; they enjoyed fishing, hunting and playing ball together. And he could always talk about anything with his mother. They trusted and cared for one another. Now he lives with a friend. The biggest problems are inflation and marijuana laws. He has been charged three times with driving while impaired. The answer? He doesn't know — for either problem.

He never made decisions about an education or a job. "It just happened! Most teachers were good; some were a pain in the ass. The ideal school? The one I went to, Eastside Tech. You couldn't beat it!"

He's self-employed as a cab driver. Though the hours are long and the pay not great, he's satisfied. "I can't find a job I like any better and I've tried all kinds ... My beliefs guide me most of the time. I'm honest. I went to Sunday School until I was 15. Sometimes I pray, especially when I'm in trouble. It helps."

## Summary: Values of Downtown Youth

While the statistical correlations between types of ideology and outcomes such as educational and occupational attainment, mobility and intrinsic satisfaction are not large, the above illustrations do indicate a consistent relationship. In reality, the magnitude of the relationship is not crucial. How a person feels about life's over-arching meaning (cosmos of meaning, or belief system) may be the tiny but immensely powerful dynamic that drives a person in this or that direction.

It is clear that while downtown humanists move in the general direction of their ideals, they are not concretely committed to them in terms of status attainment. Their careers have less evident patterns than is the case for political and religious ideologues. They are apt to be swing voters in elections and in other matters they are the quiet, morally uncertain majority.

Downtown pragmatists are least of all the type to strive for clearly defined careers. They are not risk takers or entrepreneurial in blazing new trails in learning or occupation. They play it safe in the struggle for position for a variety of reasons, some highly moral and others at least slightly amoral.

At the end of the chapter, we will compare more precisely the correlations between ideological type and outcomes that affect the status and opportunities of young adults in both areas.

## Orientations and Correlates: Northtown Sketches

### *(a) Uptown Humanists*

Martha's parents came from Portugal eight years before the study began. They live in a pleasant but not extravagant home near Northend Secondary School. Her father works for the government and her mother helps part-time in Martha's pet shop. She started the business with a loan guaranteed by them. Her father had two years in college but her mother didn't go past elementary school. A close family, they encouraged Martha to stay in school as long as she wanted. After high school she studied music but one year showed that it was not for her.

She didn't really like school and stayed only because it would help get a good job. "An ideal school should relate all courses to life situations ... An education is to prepare you for life as an adult."

She is much concerned for the environment and peace, but also feels that we should be responsible for each other. The answer to these deep needs is to "be open hearted to others." Like her parents she is not interested in religion. "It gives people false hopes ... But there is a life force I call God."

Though her dreamed-of job would be midwifery, she is happy with her pet shop. "I love animals." Compared with her parents she is upwardly mobile though she is not typically entrepreneurial.

Another daughter of European immigrants who live in Northend, Lillian thinks of her family as close. "Dad's more open; mother is strict. They gave strong support in school and sometimes I discussed a career with my mother." She doesn't know how far her father went in school but her mother took Grade Twelve. She was content with that as well, in business.

Now she's a secretary and is quite satisfied. "It's OK because soon I'll be married and raise a family."

She enjoyed high school very much although she never thought about its purpose. "School was something I had to do to get a job." Her work isn't interesting but she likes the people she is with. "Beliefs guide me. They are all really religious and set my moral standards. It didn't hit me until I was 21. In Europe I saw paintings of the Lord on the ceiling of a beautiful church. I felt the Bible all around me — the presence of God. It was wonderful — a great comfort.

"The biggest problem we have is getting along with other people. The solution is to have more understanding and better communication." She doesn't think beliefs by themselves can solve problems. You have to practise them.

Katherine's people are from Poland. Her mother is a university teacher in fine art and her father was a skilled craftsman. She was close to them both until her father died; then she stayed with her mother. "All mom's people were well educated so it was natural that I go to university. I'm now reading law ...

"Education is to develop the capacity to learn, to analyze and to apply knowledge in life. Most teachers were excellent. Though they didn't discuss current affairs or careers much, that was alright as we were there to have our minds opened."

The best school would give credits for on-the-job training as well as for general subjects. "Anyone can get a good education if they work hard. The basic problem, Katherine thinks, is alienation. "How do you solve that? ... Be more friendly ... My beliefs mean a lot to me. Integrity is most important." Her parents were too busy to talk about world problems but she and her brother always have and still do.

"Religion is not important to my parents; we only go to Polish Easter services. For me it means believing in a Supreme Being. I'm still questioning it all from an intellectual viewpoint but inside I do believe."

Humanists of both genders are quite similar in values and experiences. John is an exception as he never completed a diploma due to a learning disability. His parents, of British descent but raised in this country, couldn't help him much as they had little education. "I was only interested in phys ed., music and art. The other teachers were terrible. A counsellor tried to help me but I didn't want to talk with him or anybody else ... What's the main purpose of education? To give you an idea of what you want to do ... It didn't happen for me ...

"When mother and dad split up, I stayed with dad for a while but for several years I've been on my own. I drifted from one shitty job to another, barely getting enough to keep going. Recently I'm doing a little better.

"The main problem is the pressure to conform, which has always bothered me. The answer is to find a few loyal friends and to stand up for a fair shake for everybody ... Beliefs guide me usually but it's hard to see how they fit in with the kind of work I do ... I'm old-fashioned. A guy should be responsible, decent and honest."

John's mainstay is a few old school buddies. "We get together about once a month in the country, by a campfire or beach, drink a little beer, sing a few songs and talk a lot."

Peter's people, from Greece, are close-knit. Though with little education themselves, they encouraged Peter to plan on university. After two years of pre-med courses, he decided medicine was not his future. Now he works temporarily at furniture finishing until he decides what to do. He'd like to get married but is waiting until he decides on a career "with a challenge and good pay."

"I have two main concerns — better morality and an economy where everyone has a chance to make a living ... I'm not sure how this can be done, though I tend towards socialism. I'm not active politically ... I have a pretty strong personal faith. But the churches are too wealthy and don't help the masses. They're really not needed in a prosperous country like Canada. The best way to deal with these problems is to develop more concern for our fellow man ...

"High school was superficial though one teacher is my role model. A good school would stress career planning early and have specialization start in Grade Ten. One purpose is to develop self-reliance and discipline ... I play drums in a band ... that might lead to a career!"

## *(b) Uptown Political Ideologues*

These people advocate political action to deal with the major issue they identify. They tend to have concrete information and a strong commitment to resolve public problems and this carries over into clear notions about education and employment. More than most humanists they are upwardly mobile or at least achieve levels as high as those reached by their parents. The degree of personal involvement in politics varies. In the uptown sample, political ideologues are fewer than cohorts who take other normative positions.

Andrew unhesitatingly picks as the major human issue the use of complex technology to control social and personal development. Political policy and program is the best way to solve the problem. His studies and choice of career are based on this conviction. He is preparing at university to be an urban planner and intends to be an activist. "I'm a bicycle anarchist ... Small is beautiful ... A society based on high technology, wasteful consumption and the intensive use of energy will destroy itself." He hopes to help make better cities.

Andy comes from a highly placed family; both his parents are professors. His grandparents immigrated from Europe. He was surrounded during childhood and youth by ideas, discussions, books and journals. In a large home there was lots of space for studying. He thought of his parents as close friends; he could talk with them and trust them.

He was pleased with his high school teachers and enjoyed school, though he said that counsellors were biased in some ways. "Why did they assume that I would become a professional just because my parents are?" The purpose of an education is to give credentials, and also to provide a grounding in maths, science, literature and history. "The ideal school," he thinks, "should encourage each individual to make his or her own decisions. While the basics of each subject should be taught there should be greater effort in putting it all together."

His values are plain and he tries to practise them. For example, he belongs to the "Reform Metro" movement. His people do not go to church and he is "a complete atheist."

Ron is also a political ideologue but is not so involved as Andy. The top issue is world peace, and it will take political diplomacy and democracy to attain it. Apologetically, he admits that he doesn't belong to a group working toward this end. Further, he isn't as innovative as Andy. He is following his father's footsteps in taking a business course at college and starting as a salesman. He is pleased with the company and has had several promotions. He is chiefly interested in the quality of the job but he can afford to be choosey as he has a good income.

"For me, education means getting a basic understanding of life, learning to cooperate and attaining self-satisfaction ... The school ideally should be more structured than the old credit system, where you could drop a subject if you didn't like it, however important it was." He tries to practise his beliefs. Though the family attends church, he isn't a regular worshipper now. "The church lays out basic principles and it's up to each of us to work them out."

## (c) Uptown Religious Ideologues

The minority of the sample whose central values are religious have, as well, strong commitments to careers and upward striving. The general case for the relation of religious belief to ethical behaviour, under certain conditions, has been made elsewhere (McCready and Greeley, 1976; Weber, 1905; Crysdale, 1991, ch. 7, pp. 98-100).

Louise is a good example. Her father, a lawyer, is an enthusiastic church member. "He took us five children to church every Sunday — which I resented in my teens. My mother consistently practises Christian morality; she is loving, patient, helpful, forgiving." Louise started university with the intention of following her father's profession but after a year she realized it was not her choice and left the program. This had a traumatic effect; she was deeply depressed and worked for a year while trying to get her life together.

"Faith and loving support from the family helped me. When I switched to a business program a great load was lifted ... Now I know my potentials. I know who I am and what I want to do. I'm over my identity crisis ... I also fell in love but he didn't want to spend his life with me. It was painful. You have all this emotion but it's not logical. That's over, too ...

"When you have a good education you're smoother around the edges. You can reason. You know your possibilities and limitations. An education is not even chiefly knowledge; it's the ability to reason, to interpret what one learns ...

"Extra-curricular things helped me to stay and work hard. Histories, maths, literature were not things apart. Knowledge became integrated. I came into my own. I am an achiever.

"Beliefs strongly affect my studies and work, as well as personal relations ... You can't have commerce without morality. The most urgent problem is to have business, government and families behave ethically ... At university the most interesting people are the outcasts who question their education — not how it helps get a job but how much it helps us understand the real world ... A good school encourages this critical yet positive approach ...

"The best way to tackle the problem of ethics in business and everywhere is to practise humanistic idealism — respect, honesty, equality of opportunity. But there's something more.

"I honestly believe in God ... You can't always depend on yourself or others. If family and friends are not there I reach out to God ... The only doubt I have is about the place of the church. I know it's needed but I'm not sure just how it fits in for me ... This all affects my work. In starting a career, I know I can do well, if I apply myself. I'm really trying."

Tony, with an Italian Catholic upbringing, thinks that the biggest problem people face is to achieve peace, not only between nations but also within themselves. The one belief that will solve this problem is the rule, "Love thy neighbour as you love yourself." An outgoing, happy person, he is also very ambitious. His father owns his business, and Tony wants to get into the same line but in a different company. He's taking college courses evenings while working in the days to prepare for a better job.

He left school after Grade Twelve, which he saw later was a mistake. "Most of my friends were leaving, so I thought I would too. I'd had enough at that time. I wanted badly to make money to buy a car, date girls. Two friends left after Grade Ten and had money ... Just the thought of being in the working world, having a job, being somebody. But the level I'm working at now isn't good enough. They want university graduates at higher levels; yet I understand that the college course I'm taking is just as good ...

"What's education mean to me? It's more than just to get a job. It's to meet your own needs and prepare you for life. It sets a pattern ... getting up in the morning and being on time. But as well, it teaches you to think. Maths and accounting help particularly but the other subjects give you a background ... The perfect school would have smaller classes — ours were huge. There should be more discipline but also interest in you — love, caring. Co-education is a distraction, but I like having girls around ... Teachers should try harder to relate to teenagers."

Tony's beliefs affect his actions very much. As a Catholic he was taught to have respect for others, to be honest and decent. He is going through a time of doubt but he's certain of his faith in the long run. "Religion is organized so that there is a group of believers and there is doctrine to guide you. It's also personal and intimate. I'm not too strict and some things I don't agree with. But it worked for my parents and it will work for me, too."

### *(d) Uptown Pragmatists*

Uptown non-ideologues are not inclined toward causes. Not that they are immoral or amoral; simply, they are individualists who are skeptical of the wider world with all its institutions. They move one way or another in commitments, including careers, depending on how the wind blows. For example, Jim is in his honour year in philosophy. He is working part-time and summers for a small computer software firm and has moved into higher levels with experience. He has surpassed his parents in education and position, His father, born in England, went through the equivalent of Grade Eleven and his ambitious mother has just finished university by part-time study. He was not close to them; there was little affection at home.

"The biggest problem is the paltriness of many people. They're out of touch with real things ... we're losing the individual ... The solution? There's no panacea ... I'm interested in religion but don't see how it might solve problems."

Jim and his brothers grew up surrounded by books at home. They once counted 2,000 of them. His oldest brother is an environmental activist; he has a Ph.D. He helped start Pollution Probe. There were many discussions about public issues. "Mother is an aggressive socialist. Father is quiet but is the boss when decisions must be made ... I moved out during second year at university and live with my girlfriend ... At last I've found love and happiness ... (He and his friend beamed).

"The purpose of education is to inform you. It permits me to earn money and use it for my own pleasure ... I love to travel ... I don't particularly like to work but it's necessary and computers can be fun. The firm offered to pay half the cost of a computer science course but I turned them down. I don't like to feel obligated ... Coming back to religion, it doesn't mean a thing to me in daily life. Morals are always changing."

Alex has a very different background but has a similar, detached view of the world ... His father was an apprentice tradesman in Europe after six years at school and his mother didn't go past elementary school. "I quit Grade Twelve," says Alex, "because I felt like a dummy. I was the first in our crowd to leave. I liked tech courses; those teachers were great ... The ideal school would have everyone in work-study programs. Then you'd see why knowledge is important and how to make it work ...

"The most important issue," in Alex's view, "is the economy and the best way to help would be to lower taxes ... But I'm not involved. I sit back and let others solve problems. I've no time for it.

"Ideals? Dad was a Roman Catholic and the family went Christmas and Easter. Mom never went ... Why do you ask these questions? ... I'm happy I don't have to go. I believe in God; that's something to hold on to. But how is that related to morals?"

After he had drifted from job to job, his brother offered Alex work in his small design shop. He likes drafting and does the purchasing. His main satisfaction is with the work but he likes the money as well.

Leona is a border-line pragmatist. A native-born Anglo-saxon, she withdrew from school because of an emotional problem at home but returned to college and is taking a course in social work. Both parents had little education. "They encouraged me to stay in school but weren't able to help much ...

"The major issue is environmental damage. People must have more understanding before it can be corrected ... I'm not in any group to do anything about it. I keep to myself and do things on my own. My code is to be fair and reasonable ... Religion is important. My parents go to church but they're hypocrites. Religion is a crutch for many people. It can be positive if lived. I myself don't worship. I just do the best I can ... Social work is worth while ...

"Secondary school is too rigid. There should be more choices and classes are much too large ... Education should prepare you for life and teach skills ... There should be closer ties between schools and work. Now they're worlds apart."

Marilyn is a classic pragmatist but a strongly moral one as well. She is a part-time swim instructor, finds it interesting and can think of no other job she'd rather have. Her father went to a military academy in Rumania and her mother took Grade Ten in Canada. She herself left after Twelve, went back and quit again. Her life fell apart at age 16, the culmination of childhood neglect and abuse.

"My sisters and I were slapped around when father was in a drunken rage. We were terrified ... I can't remember ever being praised. They were always critical ... didn't try to understand us. When they lectured or punished us, which was often, they yelled at us to keep quiet ... When I retreated to a solitary place to study and think, mother would snap, 'You're always at that stupid library.' School mates didn't help. They laughed at me because I had a funny name.

"Mother was inconsistent, illogical, incommunicative. She couldn't answer my urgent questions because she was so inhibited ... I feel sorry for her now that I understand her problems. She was good with us when we were small but didn't know how to handle us when we were growing up.

"I got help at school. A teacher noticed that I wasn't well and sent me to the doctor. He put me in hospital ... It was so peaceful I didn't want to go home. He brought in a social worker who referred me to a psychiatrist.

I was suffering a deep depression and had an ulcer. They were very helpful and I gradually improved ... The vice-principal arranged for a table for me in the library where I could study. I had to sign in and out ... he kept track and encouraged me. Later the social worker got my parents to see a doctor and he told dad that he was drinking himself to death. So he stopped ...

"I came to really enjoy life when I fell in love with a good man, a salesman ... We were married and have one child ... he talked me into going to take courses and to work as a swim instructor ... He gave suggestions on how to meet problems and how to improve my skills in dealing with people ... He, too, had been rejected by his father but got along well with his mother ... He was so accepting and sensitive ... gave me time ... and love ... tried to protect me ... This saved me when I was 19 ... Teachers have no idea what some kids go through.

"About education, there are two kinds — school and life experience. There should be more life experience in the school, including work programs ... My beliefs guide me. I believe strongly in God. We were raised Catholic but I don't agree with all of it ... My parents went to church and sent us to Sunday School but they didn't know how to practise it. At Catholic school I learned that you can talk with God. When I can't talk with anyone else, even my husband, I confide in God." The main issue, according to Marilyn, is getting along by yourself. She has good reason for being, in this sense, a pragmatist. But she is an idealistic, religious one.

## Summary: Values of Uptown Youth

The same tendencies of each ideological type toward patterns of adaptation to work prevail among uptown as well as downtown youth. The most obvious difference is the level of attainment. Uptown youth tend to start at higher social strata and remain there in general, regardless of value orientation. Hence, while uptown humanists show the same aptitude for good social intentions as cohorts downtown, they also are relatively uncommitted to education and careers; but they go further in school and have higher job status than downtown humanists.

Uptown political ideologues, while fewer than downtown, have a better understanding of political process and some take leading roles. Their ideals sometimes have an effect on their striving in education and employment, whereas this course is not so open to less affluent cohorts downtown.

Religious idealism in Northend is more widespread than in Eastside and it carries over into greater success at school and work, though downtown religious ideologues also are more strongly committed to studies and employment than are humanists or pragmatists.

Pragmatists in Northend, like those in Eastside, tend to be loners and underachievers. They often had unsatisfying relations with parents and missed out on adult models; they usually didn't have clear career hopes or experiences. Like nearly all youth, they do have codes of behaviour but these are more individualistic than those of others and are subject to change under pressure. Flexibility and expedience are typical.

Patterns of attainment in relation to values are generally similar for women and men. The fact that more women uptown are religious ideologues is a reflection of gender tendencies in that subculture. It is also related to the stronger sense of inward control that is typical of middle-class women, compared with their working-class counterparts. Downtown a higher proportion of women than men are pragmatists, which suggests apathy and resignation, a result partly of social deprivation.

## Mobility Outcomes, by Ideological Type

Because the relations between values and outcomes affecting careers and lifestyle are too complex for simple analysis in descriptive terms, we summarize them statistically in Table 7–3.

The outcomes shown in the table, which relate to status attainment, are educational level reached, occupational attainment and regularity in career line. Among *downtown* youth, humanists and pragmatists fall behind those committed to religious ideals. Twenty-four percent of humanists and 30 percent of pragmatists have reached post-secondary education, compared with 50 percent of religionists. There is a similar spread between these groups in job attainment. The lowest proportion to have established regular, consistent career lines again occurs among pragmatists; next lowest are humanists. Career regularity is most common among religionists, followed by political ideologues. We may conclude that the good intentions of humanists and the expedience of pragmatists are not conducive for striving upward, as is the case for those with firm ideal commitments.

The same is true for the *middle-class uptown* sample. Again the indicators for transitional "success" are stronger among youth with clearcut ideological convictions. For example, 100 percent of religion-oriented and politics-oriented youth have post-secondary education and all religionists have better than average jobs. Both these types have career regularity.

### Table 7-3: Career Outcomes by Ideological Type, Downtown and Uptown Young Adults, In-depth Interviews (Percentages)

|  | Educational Attainment | Occupational Attainment | Career Regularity |
|---|---|---|---|
|  | (Some Post-secondary) | (Score of 50 or Higher, Blishen Scale) | (Only One Job Type Since Graduation) |
| **Downtown** |  |  |  |
| Humanist Ideologue | 24 | 18 | 59 |
| Political Ideologue | 20 | 17 | 67 |
| Religious Ideologue | 50 | 50 | 83 |
| Pragmatist | 30 | 20 | 53 |
| All Downtown Cases | 29 | 22 | 58 |
| **Uptown** |  |  |  |
| Humanist Ideologue | 73 | 73 | 55 |
| Political Ideologue | 100 | 67 | 100 |
| Religious Ideologue | 100 | 100 | 100 |
| Pragmatist | 60 | 27 | 47 |
| All Uptown Cases | 74 | 59 | 62 |

(Numbers: Downtown, 65; Uptown, 34.)

Their commitment in integrative belief systems carries over into preparation for adult employment.

The ethos of privilege among uptown youth is evident when we compare indicators of *transitional success* for total samples for the two areas. Northend youth are better educated, have better early jobs and slightly more regular career lines.

The ties between values and attainment are clearly indicated in this chapter. Statistical correlations are weak because of low numbers, but the ties are firmly in place. One reason we were not able to establish them statistically is that it did not occur to us early in the project that only by specifying ideological commitment could the linkage be traced significantly. Future studies may take this into account.

Researchers are hampered by the paucity of studies on value correlates of transition, by the complexity of the concepts and by the high cost of longitudinal enquiry. Behind these obstacles is the chronic inadequacy of research funding by public and private sources. Meanwhile, employers interviewing applicants for high level positions continue to surprise them by enquiring into their convictions, leisure-time activities and overall goals. The persistence of this line of enquiry by employers and agencies is a clue to something they know that many researchers seem to have missed.

*"Replace the engine? No problem!" (S. Crysdale)*

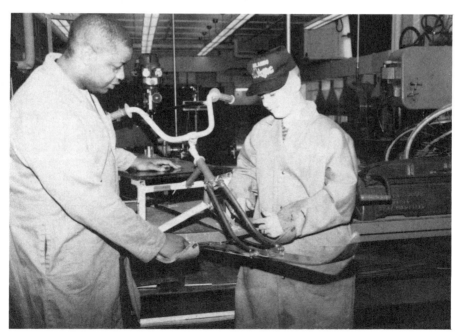

*"Let's make a snowmobile. Power it with a small motor. And then the tracks. All in a day's welding." (S. Crysdale)*

*Library session is something else! (S. Crysdale)*

*Making a doll out of a dummy. Pure magic! (S. Crysdale)*

# 8

# Summary, Conclusions and Recommendations

In passage to adult work youth respond to the socio-cultural environment, with its socialization experiences, in ways that lead to more or less stable, ranked positions. The principal indicators of rank are education, occupation and income. This chapter summarizes the process in Eastside, a downtown, working class area, and Northend, an uptown, middle class area. It presents indicators of background, socialization and outcomes in successive stages of adolescence. The chapter draws general conclusions and makes recommendations for educators, youth, employers and policy makers to improve passage through school into work.

## Summary

### *Problem and Purpose*

The focal problem is disjunction between family, school and workplace in a downtown, working class area which results in the disordered entry of a majority of youth into the world of work. A dramatic instance is the high rate of school drop-out. Nearly two-thirds of downtown youth leave school after reaching the age of 16 without having completed even a two-year program; this rate is two and one-half times that of predominantly middle-class areas in the suburbs. As a result, approximately half of young people in both areas altogether, some with high intelligence and good performance records, enter the job market without realistic goals or useful skills. Many soon experience unemployment, frustration and alienation. The situation is chronic and widespread; approximately one half of Canada's one and a half million unemployed are under the age of 25. Yet thousands of skilled jobs have insufficient qualified applicants.

The Eastside Youth Project began in 1969 after a feasibility study consulted area youth, parents, teachers, employers and community service agencies. Its purposes were, first, to study the process by which youth move through secondary school into work; second, to devise, implement and evaluate an intervention program to help youth cope with transition; and third, to improve the interaction between the chief agents of socialization during the status passage. Activities were based on the community development principle that participants, with assistance from staff, should identify goals and obstacles and decide on appropriate programs.

The research design is a field experiment in which samples of the youth population were interviewed before and after the intervention program. By controlling background and other variables, we drew inferences concerning the effectiveness of the program in meeting its objectives.

The first interviews took place in the summer and autumn of 1969, the sample representing graduates from the senior elementary school in the downtown area over a three-year period, ranging in age from 13 to 15. They were divided into two matched groups: the experimental and control groups. The first were encouraged to take advantage of the intervention programs and about one-half did so for over one year; the control group took the paths normally open to adolescents in the community.

The intervention included a work experience program for those 16 years or over — working for pay one day a week, for which they were excused from school, tutoring at home, a drop-in centre, counselling about school and work, assistance in getting and keeping part-time jobs, monthly home visits by staff, group sports, and cultural and recreational events and trips.

Three years later, in mid-adolescence, the downtown samples were interviewed again and a new uptown control group were also interviewed to provide base data from a middle class area. They matched the downtown samples in critical structural attributes. Further interviews took place two years later when members of the sample were in late adolescence and four to five years still later when they were young adults, between 23 and 25 years or age. By this time many had married and had moved to other parts of the city. Through diligent tracing, interviewers were able to complete schedules for 60 percent of the total sample during late adolescence. In view of their mobility and intense activity, this is a remarkably high completion rate. A sub-sample of 99 young adults from both areas completed in-depth interviews. Field work continued to 1985 and analysis and reporting ensued.

### *Background and Early to Mid-Adolescence*

During mid-adolescence of the youth sample, downtown families had mean incomes less than half those of uptown families. At that time no

## 8 / Summary, Conclusions and Recommendations

downtown father was a professional, manager or owner, while more than half of uptown fathers were. No father downtown had attended university, compared with one in five uptown; in addition, one in eight of the latter had some non-university post-secondary education.

Youth in Eastside on average had lower IQ scores, the result of less developed knowledge and skills, according to dominant middle-class standards. While the meaning of such scores is dubious as they reflect both social experience and mental development, they were used by schools in Grade Eight, along with other factors, to sort students into school tracks that strongly affect social destination.

More than half the Eastside youth were of British stock, compared with slightly less than half of the Northend youth. The balance of the downtown group include those of French, western European, especially Greek, and Chinese background. Uptown the majority are also of mixed origin.

As youth matured from early to mid-adolescence there was a sharp rise in the proportion of those who said that no one had influenced their plans for education and work. The influence of teachers declined more than that of parents.

More uptown youth took part in voluntary organizations than downtown, especially attending church. Over one-third of the Northend sample said that they had a career model, against less than one-quarter of the Eastside groups.

The fateful sorting of students for social destinations, at the end of Grade Eight, tracks them into the five-year academic programs or shorter technical, commercial or vocational programs. The former opens the way to university, community college and higher status jobs. Downtown, 45 percent of students were tracked into the academic program, compared with 66 percent of uptown students. The chief criteria for selection, IQ scores and elementary average marks, which are now disfavoured, were more closely adhered to uptown than downtown.

The educational aspirations or hopes of downtown youth fell in mid-adolescence and remained constant through late adolescence. The hopes of uptown youth were higher than those downtown in mid-adolescence and escalated in late adolescence.

The actual expectations or plans of most youth were lower than their hopes. By late adolescence, almost four of ten in the downtown experimental group planned to go beyond high school, not quite so many of the downtown control group had such plans, and nearly seven of ten in the uptown sample planned to take post-secondary programs. The "gap" between aspirations and expectations was smallest for the affluent uptown group, largest for the downtown control group and part-way between for the experimental group. Only one-fifth of the downtown sample achieved marks of 70 percent or higher by mid-adolescence, compared with over one-third of their uptown cohorts; over one-quarter failed, compared with one in 14 uptown.

The self-confidence of Eastside youth fell slightly between early and mid-adolescence. But by late adolescence, downtown youth, particularly the experimental group, and uptown youth became much more confident, six out of ten in both areas recording high scores.

Youth of non-British origin in Eastside, compared with those of majority origin, were much more hopeful, expecting to go beyond high school and to get high status jobs. They also got better marks. But in Northend, the British origin youth had higher hopes and plans for education and work, and did slightly better at school.

### *Late Adolescence*

By their twentieth birthday the contrast in prospects for youth from the two areas was stark. More than six of ten Eastside youth had dropped out without completing any high school program, double the rate for Northend youth. Almost four of ten downtown had gone no further than Grade Ten, against only one of 18 uptown. The most common reason given for completing secondary school was to get a good job.

The reason given most frequently for leaving was dissatisfaction with school; next in both areas was boredom.

Factor analysis of the downtown sample showed that *Grade Nine* average marks and later grade averages were significantly related to school completion. IQ scores during high school and average marks during Grades Seven and Eight *were not* significantly related with high school performance. Elementary IQ scores and marks, however, *were* strongly related with selection for school track. That the two main criteria used for tracking — elementary IQ scores and marks — were not related to later performance, raises serious doubts about their validity for separating students in Grade Eight into secondary programs that enable some but not others to enter post-secondary education.

Another finding with important consequences for policy is that in the downtown sample, school track is only weakly related with high school performance, judged by marks and completion. This challenges the widely held assumption that the academic program by itself is superior to others

## 8 / Summary, Conclusions and Recommendations

in preparing students for further education and employment. Other less well observed factors are at work to either benefit or obstruct youth's transition to work.

In spite of longer employment, only one in five downtown late adolescents held skilled blue collar, white collar or better jobs, compared with over one-third of their uptown cohorts. They had a harder time finding jobs, were much more apt to be unemployed, were four times more likely to be without job training of any kind, and were more apt to have negative attitudes towards their jobs. Job security for most downtown youth did not improve in three years and only one-quarter of them advanced in job level.

Among downtown youth working full-time by the age of 21, those who had completed high school were somewhat more likely than drop-outs to have increased self-confidence. Boys were slightly more apt than girls to be more confident than before. Being in the experimental group raised self-confidence. More minority ethnic young people grew in confidence during late adolescence than those of British origin.

### *The Intervention Programs*

Among the Eastside youth drawn for the experimental group, nine of ten accepted invitations to participate. About one-half continued to be active for more than one year.

Tutoring was sought by youth from higher than average income families, though their fathers had low status jobs. They had above average intelligence scores, were apt to be girls, and prior to the program had lower self-confidence. Eighty-three percent improved grades in the tutored subjects.

The programs helped measurably by mid-adolescence those who were active for a year or longer, in school completion, smoothness of transition to work, and self-confidence. This was particularly the case for girls, those with British-origin, those from low income homes, and those with high intelligence scores. By late adolescence, active participants also had slightly better full-time jobs than downtown cohorts.

The same sub-groups also were helped in having a smooth passage into employment. Nine of ten girls actively involved said they had no problems, compared with six of ten in the downtown control group. The largest gains in self-confidence occurred among active participants who had either high or low intelligence scores.

Participants evaluated the project in mid- and late adolescence. In the earlier survey, seven of ten said that it had helped them complete school or stay longer. In the later evaluation six of ten still felt that the project had been of some or great help. These assessments included youth who had not been active.

The Student Employment Program (prototype for later Cooperative Education programs) placing applicants in part-time jobs related to education, was most effective in preparing youth for transition into work. It was highly rated by youth, parents, participating teachers and employers.

The long-term stimulus of the project is evident in the larger proportion who later continued post-secondary education, one in five, in contrast to those from the Downtown Control Group, one in seven of whom were still studying. This is before taking account of intensity of participation; a larger proportion of those most active continued later in education and training.

Predictive models were constructed in Chapter 6 to explain how educational and job levels were attained in the two areas and how work satisfaction differed. Major sources of *educational level* in the downtown sample as a whole were, in order of importance, marks in Grades Nine and Ten, educational expectation at that time, school track, and IQ score. The model differed uptown, where track was the most important causal factor, followed by school performance in Grades Nine and Ten, and job expectation at that time, during mid-adolescence.

Different selection patterns operated in the two areas. Downtown, early disadvantages, abundantly documented in Chapters 2, 3 and 4, continued to plague youth, particularly in low marks in Grades Nine and Ten, lower expectations, over-representation in terminal, short tracks, and lower IQ scores. Individual effort and mobility were "conditioned" by institutionalized handicaps at home and school. In contrast, uptown youth had more range for "contest mobility" due to their wider placement in the academic track, along with higher performance in Grades Nine and Ten and the allure of good jobs down the road.

The regression models for *job level* in Chapter 6 support the above generalizations. While in both areas educational level strongly affects job attainment, track again becomes dominant uptown. Youth in the academic stream there have high educational and job expectations a few years hence, and this carries them beyond the low, temporary jobs they hold while still studying. Girls in both areas surpass boys in high occupations, but downtown the practice of holding girls in low-authority, white-collar levels strongly conditions their prospects.

## 8 / Summary, Conclusions and Recommendations

*Girls* in both areas are challenging traditional male dominance in education and employment. Uptown, however, they are breaking out of the stereotypical pattern of subservient positions. *Minority youth* downtown are setting the pace for educational achievement but they have not yet gained higher than average places in job markets. Uptown they are outstripped by white Anglo-saxons in education and employment.

*General job satisfaction* at this early stage in careers is diffuse. In neither area is it related with job level or pay. More than eight of ten in the entire sample said they were satisfied and, of these, four to five of ten were very pleased with their jobs. Apparently the novelty of working full-time and supporting themselves and, in some cases, their families, is the chief consideration. For the majority in both samples, satisfaction has a future orientation. The young are persistent optimists.

*Intrinsic job satisfaction*, which arises from the quality of the work itself and expresses creativity, responsibility and self-fulfilment, has similar roots in the two areas. In Eastside it is clearly related to variables which suggest an achievement life-set: job plans, church attendance of father, school track, job level, and educational level. Preference for intrinsic satisfaction does not derive from socio-economic background directly. Women are more apt than men to stress intrinsic satisfaction; this is very strongly the case in the Northend sample.

Data gathered in in-depth interviews during young adulthood permit exploration of the impact of *values* and *beliefs* on attainment in the two areas. Chapter 7 reports that in Eastside the largest number took a pragmatic position. The second largest number were humanistic ideologues, followed by political, then religious ideologues. Uptown the pragmatists were also most numerous, followed closely by humanists then religious ideologues; political ideologues were fewest. Women tended to be overrepresented among pragmatists downtown and among religious ideologues uptown.

Young adults with strong commitments to religious or political ideology tend more than others to be upwardly mobile. This is indicated by their tendency to surpass the educational level of their parents, high expected occupational level, regular career lines, and stress on the personal benefits of education apart from its utility in the job market.

## Conclusions and Recommendations

**I.** In the years since the Eastside Youth Project, there have been major curriculum changes in most secondary schools in Ontario and across the country. Credits are now allowed for cooperative education and other work-study programs, under the joint supervision of schools and employers. The number of students who take them is growing steadily, although they still total fewer than 10 percent of high school students. Of special interest is the spread of these programs among advanced level students (Ontario Ministry of Education, 1988; Ontario Ministry of Skills Development, 1987, 1989; British Columbia Ministry of Education, 1990; Alberta Ministry of Education).

The rate of drop-out in low-income areas continues at approximately two-thirds of youth past the legal leaving age of 16. Across the board it is still roughly one-third. Most leavers experience severe difficulty in finding stable and rewarding jobs. There is no evidence that the prospects for low-income youth have improved substantially since the Eastside study in th 1970s.

In contrast, two-thirds of youth in Northend completed a secondary school program and four out of ten went on to post-secondary education. Those who enter the work world thus well equipped find better jobs, with higher pay and intrinsic satisfaction. While background variables such as intelligence and the socio-economic level of parents make an important difference in educational attainment, their effects are mainly indirect through individual choice and effort. We produced path models to show the relative strength of these variables in describing the levels young people reach at the outset of their careers.

While provincial ministries of education are now moving towards reform in transition, local Boards and schools can speed the process in community innovations. The following recommendations, growing out of the Eastside Project, are intended to help develop initiatives at local, regional and senior levels.

> *Recommendation 1:*
>
> In the light of gloomy employment prospects for the large majority of school leavers, educational authorities should develop *programs such as cooperative education* to help those whose needs are not being met. All students from Grade Eight on should take courses in careers and preparation for them. Changes should be planned with community involvement and provision for evaluation.

**II.** The Eastside Project introduced a longitudinal, intervention program in the working class area to help youth complete a suitable course of study and to move smoothly into employment. Tutoring, work experience

## 8 / Summary, Conclusions and Recommendations 111

for pay one school day per week related to school program, and career counselling were highly rated by youth, teachers and employers.

*Recommendation 2:*

Projects in work education should be introduced throughout the secondary school system. *Projects should be planned to meet the specific needs of designated areas.* An "area" might consist of the zone served by several contiguous secondary schools and feeder senior elementary schools. The initiators normally would be local or area school authorities, in concert with parents, youth, teachers and employers.

*Recommendation 3:*

(a) Each project should be *administered by a Board committee or council, which would include educators, employers, youth, parents and other resource persons.* A coordinator would be responsible to the Board through the Committee. Duties would include assistance to the committee in planning programs, overseeing selection, placement and supervision of students, and liaison with teachers and employers. (b) Services should be available for students at least one year after they leave the secondary school, either by completing a diploma or withdrawing. Support by provincial Ministries of Education, in direction and funding, is essential. Organization would be blended with existing cooperative education programs.

*Recommendation 4:*

*Programs for all Grade Six, Seven or Eight students should aim at increasing their knowledge of the work world through direct observation and simulated experience.* They should be made aware of the close connection between school performance and career prospects. They should observe and, to some degree, participate in a variety of work situations and begin to form realistic concepts of possible future roles.

For some years several European systems, for example, in Sweden and Denmark, have had career orientation programs for six to ten weeks in Grades Six to Eight either in one time block or segments.

**III.** The third purpose of the Eastside Youth Project was to facilitate interaction between the family, school and workplace so as to help youth enter work satisfactorily. This was both a strategy for planning and a result of action. We tapped a large reservoir of goodwill and practical help in the community. Experience showed that community development principles are most productive. Participation in planning and decision-making by those involved opened paths which otherwise would be closed. This feature of the project generated vitality for continuity and flexibility as times and circumstances changed.

> *Recommendation 5:*
>
> *Planning and action should be based on community development principles.* The resulting community ties help to develop the creative attitudes and social skills that are essential for productive programs. Agencies that might participate include, beside schools and employers, unions, public and private service bodies, libraries, hospitals, senior citizen groups, day care centres, community colleges, universities and municipal bodies.

**IV.** In a time when some question the contribution of education, the study clearly demonstrates that, for most youth, schooling related to work is the surest route to occupational success. This applies equally for the downtown and uptown areas. The school has become the principal agent for credentializing job entrants. Educators are responsible in large measure for launching youthful careers as well as for nurturing young minds. To be relevant to the urgent needs of the young, schools must find effective ways of doing both.

Since changes cannot occur without modifying structures (Watson, 1967), one place to begin is the demonstration of alternatives in curriculum and teaching methods. In Eastside a common complaint among graduates and drop-outs from general or academic programs was that they lacked interest and practicality, while many students in applied courses said that they did not learn to think. An educated person today is at home in both the humanities and practical sciences. Moreover, the learning readiness of individuals varies with time and conditions.

> *Recommendation 6:*
>
> Curricula should convey a *balance of general and applied knowledge, both between subjects and within them* (Marklund, 1987). Students should also be free to *change* programs without undue penalties. It should become easier to be part-time students and to drop back in. Recurrent education should be built into planning.

## 8 / Summary, Conclusions and Recommendations 113

**V.** This study, like others, provides evidence of the important role of school tracking in determining the educational and occupational levels of youth. Even the influential background factor of intelligence, for the downtown sample, and education of father, for the uptown sample, act on attainments indirectly, through track. The academic pre-university track, with its concentration of high reaching students, creates an ethos which stimulates ambition and performance. But the social cost of segregating an intellectual elite is too high. The majority of students, having been tracked into shorter, applied programs, are handicapped by isolation from high achievers and stimulating general courses. And academic students are deprived of opportunity to apply and test knowledge in real life situations. No amount of capability and commitment on the part of teachers or students can correct the broadly negative effects of tracking (Gamoran, 1992).

In earlier times when access to higher education was scarce and the need for graduates limited, tracking may have been justified. But this study has produced evidence that it is no longer functional. International educational bodies advocate the ending of programs that set the abstract against the concrete and the privileged against the non-privileged (Faure, 1972). Instead, they propose a common curriculum, with a balance of general and applied subjects, until the first or second year of secondary school. Sweden, for example, delays specialization until after Grade Ten; then there are over twenty streams (Marklund, 1987).

*Recommendation 7:*

In view of the social and financial cost of maintaining a tracking system which demonstrably does not sort students efficiently or justly for differing educational and occupational levels on the basis of aptitude and interest, Boards and Ministries of Education should *eliminate tracking and set up curricula and structures which better serve youth in an increasingly competitive world market.* After a *common* curriculum for all students through the first or second year of secondary school, there should be a *variety of specialized programs* to prepare youth for a productive and satisfying adulthood, based on interest, aptitude and market opportunities.

# Appendices

## Appendix A:
## Young Adult Sample, Background by Area[1]
### (Percentages)

|  | Downtown | Uptown |
|---|---|---|
| *Ethnic Origin*[2] | | |
| British | 57 | 48 |
| Non-British | 43 | 52 |
| Total | (152) 100 | (105) 100 |
| *Sex* | | |
| Male | 49 | 53 |
| Female | 51 | 47 |
| Total | (178) 100 | (109) 100 |
| *Education of Father*[3] | | |
| Grade 8 or less | 55 | 22 |
| Grade 9 | 12 | 3 |
| Grade 10-11 | 21 | 14 |
| Finished High School | 8 | 29 |
| Some Post-Secondary | 2 | 12 |
| University | 2 | 21 |
| Total | (177) 100 | (107) 100 |
| *Education of Mother* | | |
| Grade 8 or less | 52 | 18 |
| Grade 9 | 12 | 4 |
| Grade 10-11 | 19 | 11 |
| Finished High School | 14 | 31 |
| Some Post-Secondary | 4 | 25 |
| Graduate, University | - | 11 |
| Total | (178) 101 | (109) 100 |

[1] Based on 1978 panel, using 1969 data, restricted to cases for which complete data were available.

[2] Ethnic origin of downtown population, 1971, three census tracts in survey: British, 68 percent; Asian-Oriental, 10; French, 9; German, 4; Italian, 3; other European, 5; total, 99 percent. From Census of Canada, 1971. Catalogue 95-751, CT-21B. By 1978 there had been a large increase of non-British people. The project sample framework was based on a block grid, with visits to every seventh unit. The more stable uptown sample closely approaches census track data.

[3] Census data show the following distribution for education, 1971, 5 years and over, downtown, less than Grade 9, 57 percent; some secondary, 24; completed secondary, 16; non-university post-secondary, none; some university, 2; university graduate, 1; total, 100 percent. Census of Canada, 1971, 95-751, CT-21B. Comparison with sample distribution is tenuous because the census includes children, which the sample does not do.

## Appendix B: Downtown Young Adults, Zero-Order (Pearson) Correlations between Selected Variables and Educational and Occupational Attainment[#]

| | 1 | 2 | 3 | 4 | 5 | 6 | 7 | 8 | 9 | 10 | 11 | 12 | 13 | 14 | 15 | 16 | 17 | 18 | 19 | 20 | 21 | 22 |
|---|---|---|---|---|---|---|---|---|---|---|---|---|---|---|---|---|---|---|---|---|---|---|
| 1. SEX | 1.00 | | | | | | | | | | | | | | | | | | | | | |
| 2. NONBRIT | -.04 | 1.00 | | | | | | | | | | | | | | | | | | | | |
| 3. EDFATH | -.11 | -.07 | 1.00 | | | | | | | | | | | | | | | | | | | |
| 4. EDMOTH | -.12 | -.17* | .38** | 1.00 | | | | | | | | | | | | | | | | | | |
| 5. OCCFATH | -.10 | -.07 | .21* | .17* | 1.00 | | | | | | | | | | | | | | | | | |
| 6. INCFAM 69 | -.06 | -.08 | .28** | .15* | .13 | 1.00 | | | | | | | | | | | | | | | | |
| 7. CHATFT 69 | -.25** | .45*** | -.11 | -.29** | .40*** | .22** | 1.00 | | | | | | | | | | | | | | | |
| 8. CHATMT 69 | -.16 | .38*** | -.01 | -.15 | -.04 | -.20* | .54*** | 1.00 | | | | | | | | | | | | | | |
| 9. IQ 72 | -.15 | .01 | .25** | -.14* | .03 | -.02 | -.05 | .04 | 1.00 | | | | | | | | | | | | | |
| 10. SCHLTRK 74 | -.07 | .24** | .21** | -.03 | .06 | .15* | .24* | .33** | .40*** | 1.00 | | | | | | | | | | | | |
| 11. SCLPFC 72 | -.10 | .21** | .05 | -.04 | .19* | .03 | .28** | .17 | .18* | .35*** | 1.00 | | | | | | | | | | | |
| 12. EDEXP 72 | -.02 | .25** | .20* | -.01 | .05 | .02 | .14 | .35*** | .41*** | .58*** | .42*** | 1.00 | | | | | | | | | | |
| 13. JOBEXP 72 | .09 | .33*** | .15 | -.10 | .28** | -.07 | .02 | .20* | .24* | .44*** | .18* | .55*** | 1.00 | | | | | | | | | |
| 14. JOBASP 72 | .06 | .09 | -.04 | -.04 | .24** | -.05 | -.17* | .03 | .14 | .30*** | .07 | .38*** | .68*** | 1.00 | | | | | | | | |
| 15. CHATSF 72 | .13 | .21* | -.06 | -.20* | -.16 | -.08 | .23* | .30** | -.07 | .12 | .22* | .20* | .17* | .11 | 1.00 | | | | | | | |
| 16. SELFCNF 78 | -.22* | .10 | .13 | .03 | .15 | .17* | .08 | -.30** | .09 | .16 | .09 | .04 | .23** | .17* | .07 | 1.00 | | | | | | |
| 17. IDEOLY 78 | .01 | .17* | .12 | -.06 | -.11 | -.08 | .14 | .04 | -.12 | .01 | -.03 | -.03 | -.09 | .10 | .18* | -.01 | 1.00 | | | | | |
| 18. EDATT 78 | -.02 | .25** | .20* | -.04 | .12 | .05 | .16 | .27** | .45*** | .57*** | .55*** | .63*** | .43*** | .32*** | .23** | .07 | .03 | 1.00 | | | | |
| 19. JOBATT 78 | .28** | .04 | .02 | -.11 | .12 | .12 | .03 | -.18* | .14 | .29*** | .35*** | .31*** | .32*** | .13 | .13 | .05 | .15 | .45*** | 1.00 | | | |
| 20. WKWAGE 78 | -.46*** | .01 | .08 | .06 | .15 | .07 | .07 | .05 | .16 | .20* | .09 | .10 | .22** | .03 | -.10 | .17* | .23** | .11 | .12 | 1.00 | | |
| 21. JOBMOB 78 | .08 | .06 | -.16 | -.15 | .00 | .04 | .21* | .04 | .03 | .11 | .11 | .10 | .25** | .05 | .14 | .05 | -.08 | .08 | .34*** | .09 | 1.00 | |
| 22. INT/EXSAT | .06 | .05 | .02 | -.05 | .14 | -.12 | .33** | .17* | .20* | .27** | .17* | .13 | .37*** | .19* | .01 | .06 | .04 | .24** | .26** | -.01 | -.09 | 1.00 |

Relationship between two variables is
* significant at the .05 level.
** significant at the .01 level.
*** significant at the .001 level or better.
# Includes only cases for which there are 1978 data.

## Appendix C: Uptown Young Adults, Zero-Order (Pearson) Correlations between Selected Variables and Educational and Occupational Attainment[#]

| | 1 | 2 | 3 | 4 | 5 | 6 | 7 | 8 | 9 | 10 | 11 | 12 | 13 | 14 | 15 | 16 | 17 | 18 | 19 | 20 |
|---|---|---|---|---|---|---|---|---|---|---|---|---|---|---|---|---|---|---|---|---|
| 1. SEX | 1.00 | | | | | | | | | | | | | | | | | | | |
| 2. NONBRIT | -.10 | 1.00 | | | | | | | | | | | | | | | | | | |
| 3. EDFATH | -.01 | -.09 | 1.00 | | | | | | | | | | | | | | | | | |
| 4. EDMOTH | -.09 | -.15 | .59*** | 1.00 | | | | | | | | | | | | | | | | |
| 5. OCCFATH | -.08 | -.10 | .37*** | .34*** | 1.00 | | | | | | | | | | | | | | | |
| 6. INCFAM 69 | -.05 | -.19* | .17* | .21* | .37*** | 1.00 | | | | | | | | | | | | | | |
| 7. IQ 72 | .05 | .27** | .12 | .16 | .00 | .22* | 1.00 | | | | | | | | | | | | | |
| 8. SCHLTRK 74 | .18* | -.08 | .28** | .21* | .08 | .14 | .47*** | 1.00 | | | | | | | | | | | | |
| 9. SCLPFC 72 | .36*** | -.09 | .07 | -.04 | .06 | -.10 | .49*** | .28** | 1.00 | | | | | | | | | | | |
| 10. EDEXP 72 | -.06 | -.03 | .13 | .15 | .08 | .12 | .43*** | .39*** | .34*** | 1.00 | | | | | | | | | | |
| 11. JOBEXP 72 | .26** | .03 | -.06 | .05 | .09 | .01 | .39*** | .43*** | .27** | .51*** | 1.00 | | | | | | | | | |
| 12. JOBASP 72 | .14 | .10 | -.09 | -.02 | .02 | -.19* | .14 | .29*** | .31*** | .42*** | .74*** | 1.00 | | | | | | | | |
| 13. SELFCNF 78 | -.15 | .11 | -.05 | .01 | -.04 | .12 | -.12 | -.09 | -.15 | -.13 | .19 | .09 | 1.00 | | | | | | | |
| 14. IDEOLOGY 78 | .09 | -.07 | .05 | -.10 | -.23* | .07 | .05 | .01 | -.03 | .00 | .01 | -.03 | -.04 | 1.00 | | | | | | |
| 15. EDATT 78 | .19* | -.12 | .07 | .09 | .13 | .06 | .36*** | .50*** | .43*** | .29** | .38*** | .24** | -.08 | .07 | 1.00 | | | | | |
| 16. JOBATT 78 | .27** | -.14 | -.01 | .08 | .04 | -.13 | .03 | -.14 | .24** | .14 | .02 | .19* | -.15 | -.01 | .31*** | 1.00 | | | | |
| 17. WKWAGE 78 | -.31*** | -.11 | .04 | .17* | .06 | .02 | -.24** | -.25** | .00 | .02 | -.10 | .11 | .12 | -.07 | .04 | .38*** | 1.00 | | | |
| 18. JOBMOB 78 | .11 | -.02 | -.10 | .25** | -.08 | .31** | -.12 | .10 | -.03 | -.04 | -.06 | -.14 | -.09 | -.21* | .11 | .27** | .28** | 1.00 | | |
| 19. JOBSAT 78 | .13 | -.11 | .03 | .04 | -.01 | .00 | .13 | .15 | .22** | -.01 | .24** | .06 | .12 | .16 | -.01 | -.05 | -.09 | .01 | 1.00 | |
| 20. INTRSAT | .21* | .07 | .02 | -.06 | -.08 | .05 | .09 | .08 | .03 | .15 | .12 | .03 | .08 | -.02 | .11 | .03 | .00 | .16 | .00 | 1.00 |

Relationship between two variables is
* significant at the .05 level.
** significant at the .01 level.
*** significant at the .001 level or better.
[#] Includes only cases for which there are 1978 data.

# Appendix D
# Acronyms for Appendices B and C

1. SEX         Gender of respondent, male = 1, female = 2.
2. NONBRIT     British origin = 1, all others = 2.
3. EDFATH      Education of father, ascending scale.
4. EDMOTH      Education of mother, ascending scale.
5. OCCFATH     Occupation of father, ascending values.
6. INCFAM69    Total family income, 1969.
7. CHATFT69    Regularity of father's church attendance, 1969.
8. CHATMT69    Regularity of mother's church attendance, 1969.
9. IQ72        Intelligence Quotient Score, 1972.
10. SCHLTRK74  School track, highest value, academic, 1974.
11. SCLPFC72   School performance (marks), 1972.
12. EDEXP72    Educational expectation, 1972.
13. JOBEXP72   Job expectation, 1972.
14. JOBASP72   Job aspiration, 1972.
15. CHATSF72   Church attendance, self, 1972.
16. SELFCNF78  Self-confidence, 1978.
17. IDEOLY78   Ideological orientation, 1978.
18. EDATT78    Educational attainment, 1978.
19. JOBATT78   Job attainment, 1978.
20. WKWAGE78   Weekly wage, 1978.
21. JOBMOB78   Job mobility upward, 1978.
22. INT/EXSAT  Intrinsic satisfaction with job foremost.

# References

**Adams, Bert**
1967    "Interaction Theory and the Social Network," *Sociometry*, 30:1, 64–78.

**Alvi, Sabir A.**
1980    "Work Values and Attitudes: A Review of Recent Research and its Implications," *Interchange* 11: 3, 1980–81, 67–79.

**Anisef, Paul and associates**
1975    *The Critical Juncture: Realization of the Educational and Career Intentions of Grade 12 Students in Ontario*. Toronto: Ministry of Colleges and Universities.
1980    with J.G. Paasche and A.H. Turrittin
*Is the Die Cast? Educational Achievements and Work Destinations of Ontario Youth*. Toronto: Ministry of Colleges and Universities.
1982    with Norman Okihiro and Carl James
*Losers and Winners: the Pursuit of Equality and Social Justice in Higher Education*. Toronto: Butterworths.

**Armstrong, Pat and Hugh Armstrong**
1984    *The Double Ghetto. Canadian Women and their Segregated Work*, 2nd edn. Toronto: McClelland and Stewart.

**Ashton, David and Graham Lowe, eds.**
1991    *Making Their Way: Education, Training and the Labour Market in Canada and Britain*. Toronto: University of Toronto Press.

**Bachman, Gerald G. and associates**
1978    *Adolescence to Adulthood: Change and Stability in the Lives of Young Men*. Ann Arbour: Institute for Social Research, University of Michigan.

**Benedict, Ruth**
1953 "Continuities and Discontinuities in Cultural Conditioning," in Clyde Kluckholn and others, eds. *Personality in Nature, Society and Culture*, 2nd edn. New York: Alfred Knopf.

**Bibby, Reginald W. and Donald C. Posterski**
1985 *The Emerging Generation*. Toronto: Irwin Publishing.
1992 *Teen Trends*. Toronto: Irwin Publishing.

**Blau, Peter M. and Otis D. Dudley**
1967 *The American Occupational Structure*. New York: John Wiley.

**Blos, Peter**
1962 *On Adolescence*. New York: Free Press.

**Boud, David**
1985 *Reflections: Turning Experiences into Learning*. London: Kegan Paul.

**Boudon, Raymond**
1974 *Education, Opportunity and Social Inequality*. New York: John Wiley.

**Boyd, Monica, John Goyder, Frank E. Jones, Hugh McRoberts and Peter C. Pineo**
1985 *Ascription and Achievement in Canada*. Ottawa: Ottawa University Press.

**Bowles, Samuel and Herbert Gintis**
1976 *Schooling in Capitalist America*. New York: Basic Books.

**Breton, Raymond, John C. McDonald and Stephen Richer**
1972 *Social and Economic Factors in the Career Decisions of Canadian Youth*. Ottawa: Canada Manpower and Immigration.

**British Columbia Ministry of Education**
1990 *Year 2000: A Framework for Learning*. Report of the Barry Sullivan Commission. Victoria.

**Bronfenbrenner, U.**
1986 Foreword in E. Greenberger and L. Steinberg, *When Teenagers Work. The Psychological and Social Costs of Adolescent Employment*. New York: Basic Books.

## Burman, Patrick
1988     *Killing Time, Losing Ground.* Toronto: Thompson Educational Publishing, Inc.

## Burstein, M. and associates
1975     *Canadian Work Values.* Canada Manpower and Immigration.

## Buttrick, John A.
1977     *Who Goes to University from Toronto?* Toronto: Ontario Economic Council.

## Canada Employment and Immigration Commission
1983     *Learning a Living,* vol. I, *Background and Perspectives, Report of the Skills Development Leave Task Force;* vol. II, *Policy Options for the Nation.* Ottawa.
1984     *Learning for Life: Overcoming the Separation of Work and Learning.* Ottawa.

## Canada Statistics
1961     *Census Catalogue* CT–15.
1971     *Census Catalogue* 95–751, CT–21B.

## Canadian Education Association
1983     *School and the Workplace: the Need for Stronger Links.* Toronto.

## Canadian Labour Market Productivity Centre
1988     "The Changing Nature of the Canadian Labour Market: the Increased Importance of Education and Training," *Quarterly Review,* Winter, 17–23.
1990     *A Framework for a National Training Board.*

## Cicourel, A.V. and J.U. Kitsuse
1963     *The Educational Decision-Makers.* New York: Bobbs-Merrill.

## Coleman, James S.
1961     *The Adolescent Society.* New York: Free Press.
1966     *Equality and Educational Opportunity.* Washington: U.S. Government Printing Office.
1972     "How do the Young Become Adults?" *Review of Educational Research,* 42:4.
1974     *Youth: Transition to Adulthood.* Panel on Youth of the President's Science Advisory Committee. Chicago: University Press.

**Committee on Youth**
1971  *It's Your Turn*. Report to the Secretary of State. Ottawa: Information Canada.

**Connell, R.W. and associates**
1982  *Making the Difference: Schools, Families and Social Division*. Sydney: George Allen and Unwin.

**Coser, Lewis A.**
1964  *The Functions of Social Conflict*. Glencoe, Ill.: Free Press.

**Crysdale, Stewart**
1968  *Occupational and Social Mobility in Riverdale, a Blue-Collar Community*. Ph.D. Dissertation, University of Toronto.
1974  "Secondary Education and Employment in Canada," Proceedings, Conference on Education and Work, Copenhagen. Geneva: UNESCO.
"Power and Conflict as a Theoretical Perspective in the Analysis of Change in Education," paper, International Sociological Association, August, Toronto.
1979  "The Development of Individualism and Ideology among Young Adults," presenter and discussant, Conference on North American Values and Social Change, Proceedings, Université de Bordeaux III.
1991  *Families Under Stress: Community, Work and Change*. Toronto: Thompson Educational Publishing.
1993  with Nancy Mandell, "Gender Tracks: Male-Female Perceptions of Home-School-Work Transitions," in Paul Anisef and Paul Axelrod, eds. *Transitions: Schooling and Employment in Canada*. Toronto: Thompson Educational Publishing.
In press with Alan J.C. King and Nancy Mandell, *A Productive, Resilient Generation?*

**d'Amico, Ronald**
1984  "Does Employment during High School Impair Academic Progress?", *Sociology of Education*, July, 57:3.

**Deci, E.I.**
1972  *The Effects of Contingent and Noncontingent Rewards and Controls on Intrinsic Motivation*. Toronto Board of Education.

## Dhantoa, Avtar, E.N. Wright and associates
1980 "Cooperative Education, Career Education Visit and Work Experience Weeks: An Evaluation." Toronto Board of Education.

## Drost, Helmar
1986 "Is Youth Unemployment a Temporary Problem?" *Atkinson Review of Canadian Studies.* York University, 3:2.

## Duffy, Ann, Nancy Mandell and Norene Pupo
1989 *Few Choices: Women, Work and Family.* Toronto: Garamond.

## Erikson, Erik
1963 *Childhood and Society.* New York: W.W. Norton.

## Faure, Edgar, chair
1972 *Learning To Be: The World of Education Today and Tomorrow.* International Commission on the Development of Education. Paris: UNESCO.

## Ferchat, Robert
1986 "Needs in Research Investment and Education in Canada," Couchiching Conference. Ronald Anderson, *Globe and Mail,* August 13.

## Flanagan, John C. and associates
1978 *Perspectives on Improving Education.* Project Talent's Young Adults Look Back. New York: Praeger.

## Gamoran, Adam
1992 "The Variable Effects of High School Tracking," *American Sociological Review,* 57:6, December, 812-828.

## Gilbert, Sid
1979 "The Selection of Educational Aspirations," in Richard A. Carlton, L.A. Colley and Neil J. MacKinnon, eds. *Education, Change and Society.* Toronto: Gage.

## Glaser, Nathan and Anselm L. Strauss
1971 *Status Passage.* Chicago: Aldine-Atherton.

## Gold, Martin and Elizabeth Douvain, eds.
1988 *Adolescent Development.* Boston: Allyn and Bacon.

**Grant, W.T. Foundation**

1988  *The Forgotten Half: Pathways to Success for America's Youth and Young Families*. Report, Commission on Work, Family and Citizenship. Washington, D.C.

**Greenberger, E. and L. Steinberg**

1986  *When Teenagers Work: the Psychological and Social Costs of Adolescent Employment*. New York: Basic Books.

**Hall, Oswald and Bruce McFarlane**

1962  *Transition from School to Work*. Ottawa: Department of Labour.

**Hasan, Abrar and P. de Broucker**

1984  "Turnover and Job Instability in Youth Labour Markets in Canada," in *The Nature of Youth Unemployment*. Paris: UNESCO.

**Havighurst, Robert J.**

1962  *Growing Up in River City*. New York: John Wiley.

**Hekman, Susan J.**

1983  *Max Weber, Ideal Types and Contemporary Social Theory*. Notre Dame University, Indiana.

**Heinemann, H.H.**

1981  "Cooperative Education: Integrating Work and Learning," Fifth International Conference on Higher Education. University of Lancaster, England.

**Herberg, Edward**

1982  "Ethnicity and Intergenerational Education Mobility," paper at the Canadian Sociology and Anthropology Association annual meeting, Ottawa.

**Horwich, Herbert**

1980  *Social and Cultural Factors Affecting Retention at the Secondary and Post-secondary Levels in Quebec*. vol. XI, Aspirations Scolaires et Orientations Professionelles des Étudiants. Laval University.

**Hyman, Herbert**

1966  "The Value Systems of Classes: A Social Psychological Contribution to the Analysis of Stratification," in Reinhard

Bendix and Seymour L. Lipset, eds. *Class, Status and Power,* 2nd edn. Glencoe, Ill.: Free Press.

**Inkeles, Alex**
1968    "Status and Experience, Perception and Values," in John A. Clausen. *Socialization and Society.* Boston: Little, John.

**International Bureau of Education**
1973    *The Relationship between Education, Training and Employment.* Report, 34th Session. Geneva.

**Jencks, Christopher and associates**
1972    *Inequality: a Reassessment of the Effect of Family and Schooling in America.* New York: Basic Books.

**Karp, Ellen**
1988    *The Drop-out Phenomenon in Ontario Secondary Schools: A Report to the Ontario Study of the Relevance of Education and the Study of Drop-Outs.* Toronto: Ministry of Education.

**Keil, E. Theresa, D.S. Riddell and B.S.R. Green**
1966    "Youth and Work: Problems and Perspectives," *American Sociological Review,* 13.

**Kerckhoff, Alan C.**
1974    *Ambition and Attainment: a Study of Four Samples of American Boys.* Washington: American Sociology Association.

**King, Alan J.C. and J. Hughes**
1985    *Secondary School to Work: A Difficult Transition.* Toronto: Ontario Secondary School Teachers' Association.

**King, Michael, A.A. Murray and Tom Atkinson**
1979    *Background, Personality, Job Characteristics and Satisfaction with Work in a National Sample.* Quality of Life Project, Working Paper 3. Institute for Social Research, York University.

**Kohlberg, Lawrence**
1964    "The Development of Moral Character and Moral Ideology," in M.L. Hoffman and L.W. Hoffman. *Review of Child Development Research,* vol. I. New York: Russell Sage Foundation.

**Krahn, Harvey and Graham Lowe**
1993    *Work, Industry and Canadian Society,* 2nd edn. Toronto: Nelson.

1991 "Transitions to Work: Findings from a Longitudinal Study of High School and University Graduates in Three Canadian Cities," in David Ashton and Graham Lowe, eds. *Making Their Way.* Toronto: University of Toronto Press.

**Lawton, Stephen B. and Kenneth A. Leithwood**
1988 *Student Retention and Transition in Ontario High Schools: Policies, Practices and Prospects.* Student Retention and Transition Series. Toronto: Ministry of Education.

**Lenski, Gerhard E.**
1954 "Status Crystallization: A Non-Vertical Dimension of Social Status," *American Sociological Review*, 19, August.

**Lowe, Graham with David Ashton**
1991 op. cit. David Ashton.
1993 with Harvey Krahn
*Work, Industry and Canadian Society.* 2nd edn., op. cit.

**Maccoby, Eleanor E. and C.N. Jacklin**
1974 *The Psychology of Sex Differences.* Stanford: Stanford University Press.

**Harry MacKay**
1973 *A Study in Adolescent Socialization.* M.A. thesis, York University.
1978 *Inequality of Opportunity for Youth in Transition from School to Work.* Ph.D. dissertation, York University.

**Maizels, Joan**
1970 *Adolescent Needs and the Transition from School to Work.* London: Athlone Press.

**Mandell, Nancy and Stewart Crysdale**
1993 "Gender Tracks: Male-Female Perceptions of Home-School-Work Transitions," in Paul Anisef and Paul Axelrod, eds. *Transitions: Schooling and Employment in Canada.* Toronto: Thompson Educational Publishing.

**Marklund, Sixten**
1987 "School Development in Sweden," in Robert F. Lawson, ed. *Changing Patterns of Secondary Education.* Calgary: University of Calgary Press.

## Marsden, Lorna
1986  "The Unemployment of Young Canadians is Not Only About Jobs," *Atkinson Review of Canadian Studies*, 3:2, Spring-Summer. York University.

## Marsh, Herbert W.
1991  "Employment during High School: Character Building or a Subversion of Academic Goals?", *Sociology of Education*, 64:3, July, 172–189.

## McCready, W.C. and A.M. Greeley
1967  *The Ultimate Values of the American Population*. Beverley Hills, Cal.: Russell Sage.

## Mischel, W.
1970  "Sex-typing and Socialization," in F.E. Mussen, ed. *Carmichael's Manual of Child Psychology*. New York: John Wiley.

## National Commission on the Reform of Secondary Education.
1973  *The Reform of Secondary Education: A Report*. New York: McGraw-Hill.

## Ontario Ministry of Education
1988  *Student Retention and Transition: A Selection of Progam Models*. Toronto.

## Ontario Ministry of Skills Development
1987  *Out of School Youth in Ontario: Their Labour Market Experience*. Toronto.
1989  *Pathways: A Study of Labour Market Experience and Transition Patterns of High School Leavers*. Toronto.

## Ontario Teachers' Federation
1983  *The School to Work Transition*. Toronto.

## Ontario Premier's Council
1988  *Competing in the New Global Economy*. Toronto.
1990  *People and Skills in the New Global Economy*. Toronto.

## Organization for Economic Cooperation and Development
1976  *Reviews of National Policies for Education*. Canada.
1977  *Entry of Young People into Working Life*. Paris.
1984  *The Nature of Youth Unemployment*. Paris.

**Parnes, H.S., C.R. Miljus, R.S. Spitz and others**
1970, 1971, 1973
    *Career Thresholds.* U.S. Department of Labour/Manpower Administration. Washington.

**Peel Board of Education**
1987    *Survey of Cooperative Education Participants.* Mississauga, Ontario.

**Piaget, Jean and B. Inhelder**
1969    *The Psychology of the Child.* New York: Basic Books.

**Pike, Robert M.**
1970    *Who Doesn't Get to University—and Why.* Ottawa: Association of Universities and Colleges of Canada.

**Porter, Marion, John Porter and Bernard Blishen**
1973/1982
    *Does Money Matter?* Toronto: Institute for Social Research, York University. revn. Stations and Callings. Toronto: Methuen.

**Radwanski, George**
1967    *Ontario Study of the Relevance of Education and the Issue of Drop-Outs.* Toronto: Ontario Ministry of Education.

**Reitz, J.G.**
1980    *The Survival of Ethnic Groups.* Toronto: McGraw Hill-Ryerson.

**Richer, Stephen**
1979    "Sex-role Socialization and Early Schooling," *Canadian Review of Sociology and Anthropology,* 16:2.

**Richmond, Anthony H. and W.E. Kalbach**
1980    *Factors in the Adjustment of Immigrants and Their Descendents.* Ottawa: Statistics Canada.

**Roberts, Kenneth**
1968    "Entry into Employment: An Approach Toward a General Theory," *Sociological Review,* 16.

**Rosenberg, Morris**
1965    *Society and the Adolescent Self-Image.* Princeton: Princeton University Press.

## Ryrie, Alexander C.
1983  *On Leaving School*. Edinburgh: The Scottish Council for Research into Education.

## Schreiber, Daniel, ed.
1967  *Profile of the School Drop-Out*. New York: Random House.

## Sewell, William H.
1971  "Inequality of Opportunity for Higher Education," *American Sociological Review*, 36:5, October. with A.O. Haller and A. Portes.
1969  "The Educational and Early Occupational Attainment Process," *American Sociological Review*, 34:1, February, with A.O. Haller and G.W. Ohlendorf.
1970  "The Educational and Early Occupational Attainment Process: Replication and Revision," *American Sociological Review*, 35:6, December.

## Sherif, M. and C. Sherif
1965  *Problems of Youth*. Chicago: Aldine.

## Simon, Roger I. and associates
1991  *Learning to Work*. New York: Bergin and Garvey.

## Slavin, Robert E.
1990  *Cooperative Learning: Theory, Research and Practice*. Englewood Cliffs, N.J.: Prentice-Hall.

## Turner, Ralph H.
1964  *The Social Context of Ambition*. San Francisco: Chandler.

## United States General Accounting Office
1990  *Training Strategies: Preparing Non-college Youth for Employment in the U.S. and Foreign Countries*. Washington.

## Vroom, V.H.
1964  *Work and Motivation*. New York: Wiley.

## Watson, Goodwin
1967  *Change in School Systems*. Washington: National Education Association.

## Weber, Max
1930  *The Protestant Ethic and the Spirit of Capitalism*. (1905) London: George Allen and Unwin.

**Weiermair, Klaus**
1986 "Secular Changes in Youth Labour Markets and Youth Unemployment in Canada," *Relations Industrielles*, 41:3.

**Williams, Trevor H.**
1972 "Educational Aspirations: Longitudinal Evidence on Their Development in Canadian Youth," *Sociology of Education*, 45, Spring.

**Woelfel, Joseph and A.E. Haller**
1971 "Significant Others, the Self-Reflexive Act and the Attitude Formation Process," *American Sociological Review*, 36, February.

**Wright, E.N.**
1970 "Students' Background and its Relationship to Class and Programme in School," Toronto Board of Education, *Research Bulletin* 91.
1972 "Inner City Students and their Secondary School Programmes," Toronto Board of Education, *Research Bulletin* 103.

**Yinger, J. Milton**
1970 *The Scientific Study of Religion*. London: Collier-MacMillan.

**Young, Vivienne and Carol Reich**
1974 "Patterns of Dropping Out," Research Department, Toronto Board of Education.